The Great Hysteria and the Broken State

SANJEEV SABHLOK

FOREWORD BY GIDEON ROZNER

connorcourt
PUBLISHING

Published in 2020 by Connor Court Publishing Pty Ltd

Copyright © Sanjeev Sabhlok, 2020

All rights reserved. No part of this book may be reproduced or transmitted in any form or by any means, electronic or mechanical, including photo copying, recording or by any information storage and retrieval system, without prior permission in writing from the publisher.

Connor Court Publishing Pty Ltd
PO Box 7257
Redland Bay QLD 4165
sales@connorcourt.com
www.connorcourt.com
Phone 0497-900-685

Printed in Australia

ISBN: 9781922449283

Front cover design: Ian James

Front cover photo: Collins Street, Melbourne, Steve Walshe, used with permission.

Dedicated to the memory of those who should never have died during the coronavirus pandemic: many of the elderly whom our dysfunctional governments failed to protect, and the young who lost hope because of extended lockdowns and ended up taking their own life.

And to the living experience of millions of survivors (who were never at risk of dying from COVID-19) whose lifespan has been cut short because, terrorised by the hysteria drummed up by their government, they did not get – or seek to access – timely medical care for the myriads of other afflictions that are part of our human condition.

Contents

FOREWORD 7
PREFACE 9
ACKNOWLEDGEMENTS 12

1. BIG TICKET ISSUES 13
1.1 Comparing this pandemic with other pandemics. And what is its death rate? 25
1.2 Important facts about the pandemic in Australia and Victoria 29
1.3 The Victorian Government abandoned its pandemic plan the moment things heated up 31
1.4 The deaths of the elderly in Victoria that lockdowns failed to prevent 34
1.5 Government terrorism: Havoc, and potentially millions of deaths from lockdowns 35

2. OTHER PROBLEMS WITH LOCKDOWNS 41
2.1 Lockdowns are not recommended by the W.H.O. "in any circumstances" 41
2.2 Lockdowns breach many international covenants 45
2.3 Does a moral (prudential) algebra or a cost-benefit test of lockdowns tell us something different? 47

3. INNER WORKINGS OF A VIRAL PANDEMIC 53
3.1 Viruses are a part of us 53
3.2 How our body fights viruses 55
3.3 A natural vaccine to COVID-19 is probably to be found in our kindergartens 59
3.4 In sum, we humans are not defenceless against SARS-CoV-2 60
3.5 Herd immunity now likely already exists or is very close in many countries 63

4. THE BROKEN STATE 65
4.1 Alarm bells in my head when lockdowns were imposed 65
4.2 Capricious government: masks outdoors, the Police State and my resignation 71
4.3 Sliding towards authoritarian communism 75
4.4 Loss of society's moral compass 78

4.5 Loss of agency and the right to work   80
4.6 The institutions of Australia seem to be fraying at the edge   81

5. WHY DID THE VICTORIAN GOVERNMENT LOSE ITS HEAD? 83
5.1 Why did Victoria abandon its pandemic plan?   83
5.2 The Swedes followed their plan and did not buckle to the hysteria   93

6. CALL FOR ACTION: IMMEDIATE ACTIONS 97
6.1 Lift the lockdowns, open the borders and work with industry to create risk-based solutions   97
6.2 A vaccine may no longer be needed, like with all previous pandemics   98
6.3 Vaccine must not be mandatory when it does arrive   100
6.4 No mass testing   101
6.5 How concerned should we be about the long-term effects of COVID-19?   102

7. CALL FOR ACTION: LONGER TERM ACTIONS
7.1 Revoke peacetime emergency powers of all governments   106
7.2 Expunge the precautionary principle from all legislation   108
7.3 Review commonwealth powers   111
7.4 Enact a law in Victoria to criminalise public health terrorism   113
7.5 Ethics control over government advertising   113
7.6 Review the hiring and firing arrangements for the senior executive service   114
7.7 Let doctors decide the medicine they want to administer   115
7.8 Prohibit all forms of government surveillance   116
7.9 Create a Black Hat Commissioner to stop public service groupthink   116
7.10 Clarify the nature of a public servant's voice in social media   117
7.11 Large-scale working from home is unsuitable for the public service   118
7.12 Prohibit false and misleading data on cases and deaths   120
7.13 Other possible legislative measures   120
7.14 Reset the discipline of epidemiology   120

8. CONCLUSION 125

Foreword

We've been told a lot of lies about Australia's coronavirus response. You'll read about many of them in this book, but to me the biggest one has always been that 'we're all in this together'.

From day one, the coronavirus has laid bare Australia's sharp divide between the two groups my colleague Matthew Lesh has called 'inners' and 'outers'. Well-heeled 'inners' – politicians, public servants, academics and scores of rent-seekers subsisting off the public teat – have dreamed up pointless restrictions, safe in their taxpayer-funded, six-figure salaries.

The consequences of their decisions have been borne almost entirely by 'outers' – parents who've had to moonlight as teachers while struggling to hold down a job, the hundreds of thousands of Australians who've been thrown out of work, and above all, small business owners who've seen their life's work destroyed with the stroke of a pen.

And the greatest injustice is that when the catastrophic failures of Victoria's coronavirus response became clear, there were no consequences for anyone responsible. Not one public servant lost their job, not one minister was sacked. (Yes, Jenny Mikakos resigned, but that was probably more of a kamikaze exercise than a sudden pang of ministerial responsibility.)

But on 16 September, one Victorian public servant did resign. Not because he had anything to do with Victoria's ongoing coronavirus catastrophe – he didn't. Rather, Sanjeev Sabhlok quit in protest, and importantly, so that he could speak out against the government's actions. In this book, you'll find out why it was so important that he did.

As Director of Policy at the Institute of Public Affairs – Australia's oldest and largest free market think tank – I've been speaking out against lockdowns from the beginning. On 4 April, we became the first organisation in Australia to call for a 'COVID-safe' reopening, releasing an online video in which I stood in an empty Melbourne street and spoke about the terrible damage that prolonged lockdowns would do.

For this, I was derided as a dangerous lunatic, blasted on social media and slagged off by everyone from Channel Ten's Hugh Riminton to actor Sam Neill. But privately, I received hundreds of messages from people who thanked me and the IPA for saying what they, for whatever reason, could not. Since then, our position has gone from 'crazy' to mainstream, and I've kept hearing from the victims of what is unquestionably the greatest public policy failure in Australian history.

But reading this book made me realise that the Victorian government's actions weren't as bad as I thought. They are much, much worse.

In these pages, you'll get an insider's look at the failures that made this catastrophe possible. You'll learn about the way in which sensible pandemic plans based on risk and proportionality were cast aside in favour of extreme and unscientific lockdowns. You'll find out about the breakdown in the functioning of government that led to such punitive and irrational policies. You'll see how the Andrews government ignored its own legislation and possibly acted unlawfully. And you'll realise – if you haven't already – that Victoria's coronavirus response was not, as the Premier insists, based on 'the best medical advice', but the worst.

Sanjeev Sabhlok has done Australia a great service by writing this book. It is a shocking and desperately-needed wake-up call to anyone who still takes Dan Andrews' meaningless press conferences at face value.

And when future historians try to figure out how Victoria, Australia and the better part of the civilised world could descend into such an orgy of stupidity, incompetence and cruelty, *The Great Hysteria and the Broken Government* will be a vital resource.

Gideon Rozner

October 2020

Preface

On 9 September 2020 I resigned from my role as an economist in the Victorian Department of Treasury and Finance. This was not any ordinary pause in a career. It was to lodge a protest against the policies of the Victorian Government.

I explained the reasons for my resignation in a piece in the *Australian Financial Review* on 16 September 2020, entitled, "Why I quit rather than be silenced".[1] This book is a fuller exposition.

I have been keen to get this book out as soon as possible. Each day delayed, each day of unnecessary lockdowns, is one additional day of catastrophic harm to the people of Australia. Therefore, in just about ten days I have assembled the few arguments that I can muster. For sometimes, the perfect is the enemy of the good.

I hope this book will contribute to the urgent changes in pandemic policy that we need right now, as well as to the longer-term debates about the country we want to be.

At the outset, let me also provide a background about my political affiliations, which are none.

I have been a resident of Australia for 20 years and citizen for the past 15 years. I have remained strictly apolitical. It might surprise some readers that in the 2018 Victorian State elections I voted for Labor since

---

[1] Sabhlok, Sanjeev, "Why I quit rather than be silenced: Vic Treasury insider", *Australian Financial Review*, 16 September 2020. Short URL: https://bit.ly/3jhUw0Z.

Daniel Andrews, in my view at that time, deserved a second term. He was at least marginally better than Victoria's insipid opposition and had implemented small but meaningful policy reforms during his first term. He had also started a significant infrastructure build that Melbourne desperately needed.

So, the fact that I joined a protest which was held from people's homes across Victoria on 13 September 2020 with the Twitter hashtag #GiveDanTheBoot, was an expression of my anguish at his having lost the way. It is the first protest I have joined in my life. But even at that stage I did not ask Mr Andrews to go. I said that he should go *if* he doesn't reset his pandemic policies.

I hope that politicians from all sides of politics will see this book as a plea for the return of sanity. And that they will come off the pedestal from which they lecture us and, instead, share with us their detailed objectives, plans and justifications for their pandemic policies. We will then judge for ourselves whether they are doing the right thing. The disclosure of their detailed logic must also tell us precisely how many of us our governments are willing to sacrifice at the altar of the Public Health God, to save others. How many of our children precisely do we want to force into self-harm, how many young adults into depression, how many into suicide and how many into undetected cancer and heart disease, to wipe out decades off their lives?

They should also tell us which law gives them the power to take even a single additional life in this manner. In normal parlance, each and every one of these actions is a serious crime. Where exactly did we the People authorise our governments to commit mass-scale crimes in order to, allegedly, save some of us?

I also hope that anyone who is still fearful about this pandemic will gain a healthier sense of proportion and a lot of hope from this book: an assurance that we can look after ourselves and that we do not need a government to force us to look after ourselves at the point of a gun. I'm trying to say that it is not just the people of Sweden who are blessed with common sense. Even we ordinary Australians might have some.

I hope also that the people of Australia will organise to drive the reforms we need to ensure that this sorry episode does not happen again. Our journey must not end with the end of lockdowns and opening of all borders. We must keep the eye on the ball till we succeed in imposing tight restrictions on the powers of our governments.

Should this book prove to be helpful in any way or should readers wish to provide any feedback to improve my arguments, please feel free to write to me at sabhlok@gmail.com. I might take a second bite at this exposition in the future.

Perhaps this is also the place where I should add a disclaimer for anyone who accidentally stumbles into this book looking for health advice about COVID-19. This is a book purely about big picture issues. It also goes without saying that readers should independently verify any claims I make in this book upon which they wish to act.

Sanjeev Sabhlok

Melbourne, 3 October 2020

https://twitter.com/sabhlok

https://www.facebook.com/sabhlok/

Acknowledgements

I wish to thank the publisher, Connor Court Publishing, for offering me an opportunity to put on record the fuller arguments in support of my 16 September 2020 *Australian Financial Review* article.

Fortunately, I did not need to start from a blank slate. I had already authored 17 articles about the pandemic in my *Times of India* blog[2] since March 2020.

I set myself a two-week timeline for delivering the manuscript. The publisher has very ably worked overtime to ensure that this book is able to reach the people in the shortest possible time.

Some of my friends and family members, whom I have thanked privately, have assisted me over the last week in weeding out typos and providing me with structural and other insights. I want to particularly thank a new friend I have made on LinkedIn, Ms. Alexandra Chapman, who has provided me with invaluable suggestions that have helped to make this book clearer to read. Of course, any remaining obscurity is purely a failure of mine.

I must not forget to acknowledge the many wonderful people who have provided me with valuable information and insights over the past week on social media or via email, in response to my social media invitation for people's input into this book. They will recognise their voice in some of the content. In particular, I learnt a lot from these inputs about the sound policy-making principles that are embedded in our public health and biosecurity laws, as well as in international covenants. Our laws may not have failed us; our leaders did.

---

[2] https://timesofindia.indiatimes.com/blogs/seeing-the-invisible/

1

Big Ticket Issues

Common sense is the realised sense of proportion

Mahatma Gandhi

Just when we needed sane, stable and rational governments in March 2020 – at a time when mass hysteria was starting to build across the world about the coronavirus pandemic – the governments of Australia abandoned their well-thought-out published pandemic plans[3] and all the principles of risk-based management and proportionality which are embedded in our laws, to add fuel to the hysteria and confusion.

No one, not even within the government, seems to know exactly what we are trying to achieve. Are we are flattening the curve, suppressing the virus or trying to eliminate it from the face of the Earth? Or do the governments want indefinite lockdowns until everyone can presumably be jabbed by zealous police with a vaccine that is not yet available, let alone properly tested?

Daniel Andrews at least seems to have this possibility in his mind. He said this on 4 July 2020:

---

[3] Victorian Government, "COVID-19 Pandemic Plan for the Victorian Health Sector", 10 March 2020. Short URL: https://bit.ly/2FPeqSJ.

At that point we will not be returning to normal because there will be no vaccine in the weeks ahead, some argue even in the months ahead. It is a long way off. And unless and until that vaccine is developed, and then *administered to every single Victorian*, we will have to live with and embrace a COVID normal.[4] (emphasis mine.)

All prepared plans and laws have been abandoned on the basis of a hunch – playing God with the lives of 6.7 million real humans as if we are Daniel Andrews's chattel.

We must never let any politician tell us tomorrow, when they are grilled by a Royal Commission that is sure to be established, that they were "following the science". They have not followed the science. In preparing for pandemics, governments carefully consider the science. Lockdowns (on any pretext) are *rejected outright* by the science. That is why they are not in our pandemic plans.

A pandemic is no time to invent new science and ditch all the laws which insist on implementing a risk-based, proportional response. There is no law in Victoria, leave alone the world, which states: "The moment a 'scientist' comes up with a scary looking mathematical model during a pandemic, or the Premier then 'feels' like waiting indefinitely for a vaccine, everything in the Constitution, everything in the laws about proportionality – and all pandemic plans – can be abandoned".

Daniel Andrews is perfectly free to lock himself up till eternity if he wishes to wait for a vaccine. But he does not own us. He cannot control us like he controls his pet dog or cat.

Politicians cannot also tell a future Royal Commission that they dumped

---

[4] The New Daily, "Victoria's COVID crisis grows: Two more postcodes locked down, 108 fresh cases", 4 July 2020. Short URL: https://bit.ly/3ixgeg9. The video of Daniel Andrews's statement is found in a Tweet by @YellowCube7 on 3 October 2020. Short URL: https://bit.ly/3cWdmbD.

the plans because of the precautionary principle. Pandemics are a well-known and well-understood contingency and our plans had pandemics of all magnitudes fully covered. It was prudent, therefore, and in fact mandatory, for governments to follow the plans.

But I am not one of those crazy "libertarians". I would have been willing to accept all loss of freedoms, even permanent solitary confinement, if government had proven to me, after thorough analysis and scientific proofs, that there is no better way to save our species from extinction. But Daniel Andrews is never going to do that. His only justification for his policies is his personal hunch. *All* cost-benefit analyses of lockdowns that have been conducted by independent economists to date confirm that lockdowns always cause far more harm than good.

We the People are not stupid. We understand that Nature is not always our friend. From time to time, it springs unpleasant surprises. We understand that there can be unavoidable deaths from a natural cause (an Act of Nature). But we cannot – must not, and will not – tolerate, condone, or cope with public health directives that end up killing *even one additional person* (which then becomes an Act of Man: a murder, homicide, manslaughter or whatever – but definitely not a *health* measure, which is the only thing that public "health" – yes, health – directives are authorised to ensure).

There is blood – a *lot* of blood – on the hands of our political leaders and policymakers.

As Dr. Sucharit Bhakdi, the head of the Institute for Medical Microbiology and Hygiene in Germany has said, lockdowns "are leading to self-destruction and *collective suicide* based on nothing but a spook".[5] (emphasis mine.)

---

[5] "Necessary measures or mass panic", *Europost*, 26 March 2020. Short URL: https://bit.ly/345k2Ae.

We must not hesitate to call this episode by the unsavoury but accurate name it deserves: public health terrorism. As Dr Eammon Mathieson said in an interview to Reignite Democracy Australia on 18 September,[6] when practicing medicine "we don't terrorise our patients".

The lockdowns may have killed hundreds of thousands of people, if not yet millions, across the world. But this is not just about deaths that are taking place as we speak. Lockdowns will leave behind a long tail of tragedy and devastation well into the future, reducing the lifespan of the entire current generation.

We also know that Western nations, which had the capacity to organise quickly, could easily have saved most of the elderly who have died from COVID-19 in these countries (including in Victoria) if they had followed their plans and (therefore) focused mainly on the high-risk segment of the population. But they were busy spending their scarce time in getting police involved in arresting people outdoors without a masks people who face virtually no risk of death from COVID-19.

In other words, we are seeing mass-scale crime and crimes against humanity of two types: (a) crimes of commission (additional non-COVID casualties) as well as (b) crimes of omission (failure to avert preventable COVID-19 deaths). A mass-massacre.

Governments are not authorised by any law – by analogy – to burn down additional homes and kill unaffected people in order to save those who might be at risk of being engulfed in a bushfire.

* * *

Some readers might ask in bewilderment: Am I suggesting that we should have "let it rip"? Surely it was right to impose the lockdowns when panic had reached a crescendo in mid-March 2020 and everyone

---

[6] Reignite Democracy Australia, Facebook Page, 18 September 2020. Short URL: https://bit.ly/2RYh37e.

was saying that this would be another Spanish flu. Why was it wrong to have imposed lockdowns then? Shouldn't social distancing have been observed? Shouldn't people have reduced the use of public transport?

"Letting it rip" was never part of our pandemic plan. If we had followed the plan, the government would have:

- focused like a crazed hen on protecting the elderly;
- created limited and highly targeted quarantines (for a short and appropriate duration) wherever needed;
- issued recommendations about hygiene and social distancing to flatten the curve; and
- encouraged people to work from home wherever possible;

But, no, there would never have been *coercive* society-wide, untargeted lockdowns including a mass shutdown of workplaces.

What lockdowns do is to harm the overwhelming majority of the people – millions in Melbourne itself, and billions across the world – who face little risk from COVID-19 even if they were to catch it. These harms then multiply in the same magnitude – of millions, billions – till they become a crescendo that overwhelms any COVID-19 lives we might save.

After an entire year of COVID-19 (the virus started in October 2019), 99,987 persons on this planet have survived this virus out of every 100,000. In other words, just 13 have died out of every 100,000 – and most of these were very old but many of whose deaths could have been prevented had governments just focused on high-risk groups.

Regardless, it doesn't make any sense, no matter which way we look at it, for governments to harm 99,987 people out of every 100,000 in order to possibly (for that's not something that science agrees with at all) save maybe a few more.

But readers might ask: Doesn't it make sense to wait for a vaccine? We know that of the three major pandemics over the past 100 years, none ended because of a vaccine. There was no vaccine in the 1918 Spanish flu and "vaccines arrived too late in both the 1957 and 1968 influenza pandemics to make a difference".[7] The science of pandemics underpins our officially approved plans. It is for very good reasons – and not because our dim-witted policy makers of the past somehow missed this glorious, possibly Nobel prize winning "remedy" of lockdowns – that our plans do not have the provision to lock up society indefinitely while waiting for a vaccine.

Our rights to self-determination are inalienable, non-negotiable. A government can only restrain us if we commit a crime Any other restraint is not just a violation of the laws, it is a breach of the trust we have placed in our governments. We are capable of individually choosing whether we will wait for a vaccine, but waiting for a vaccine can *never* be allowed to become public policy.

* * *

A description of lockdowns I found on LinkedIn sums it up: "Lockdowns are dumb, they're [as] tunnel visioned as they are barbaric".

- Lockdowns are dumb because science does not support them.

- Lockdowns are tunnel-visioned because they ignore all other aspects of human life, including mental and physical health.

- Lockdowns are barbaric because they push us into the era in which lepers were segregated and confined.

* * *

The situation today has gone well beyond the farcical. Even the blind can

---

[7] Honigsbaum, Mark, "Revisiting the 1957 and 1968 influenza pandemics", *The Lancet*, 25 May 2020. Short URL: https://bit.ly/33kvpoX.

see that this virus is not the Spanish flu. My ballpark estimate, as I will presently elaborate, is that the coronavirus pandemic is probably around 50 times less lethal than the Spanish flu and that it could even end up being around 100 times less lethal. This is a undoubtedly a bad pandemic but it no reason to remain hysterical even now.

Moreover, we can by now be very certain that by protecting the elderly, by encouraging people to strengthen their immune system and by letting doctors administer the drugs they believe will work, the number of future COVID-19 deaths in Australia can be significantly minimised, even as we avert the colossal harms of coercive lockdowns by stopping them *right now*.

* * *

The past six months have felt surreal, with increasingly more restrictive rules coming into effect almost every week – a progression of events that someone on Twitter has called a "compliance cascade".

Like the millions of fellow Melbournians around me, I have been boxed into my home, staring at the computer screen, unwilling to go outdoors even in the short period that is permitted because I hate wearing a mask outdoors in an open park.

On my computer screen I have been seeing videos of an overzealous Victorian police force that has lost its way. Instead of catching criminals, officers of Victoria's police have been seen arresting people for the crime of not wearing a mask outdoors, putting handcuffs on a pregnant woman in her own home (as if she was going to flee in her pyjamas) and snatching the phone of an elderly lady sitting on a bench – all these brave efforts apparently to save the rest of us from the virus.

I don't think any of us wants to be saved in this way.

* * *

We all accept, no doubt with regret, that during a war there will be unavoidable civilian casualties on both sides. But in this "war against COVID", we are ourselves the collateral damage.

The Hippocratic oath says: *First, do no harm.*

Governments work hard to ensure that vaccines and medicines are tested intensively so that they will cause no side-effects, leave alone additional deaths. But when it came to lockdowns that had been widely understood in the scientific literature to be extremely harmful, there was no testing before imposing this unproven "remedy".

Extremism in the name of public health is not new. Scholars have long known that despite their Hippocratic oath, some members of the medical fraternity can on occasion become over-zealous. There is robust literature regarding widespread historical abuse of power supposedly to protect public health.

In 2009, Wendy Parmet, the Director of the Northeastern University's Program on Health Policy and Law said, "The history of public-health responses and the abuse of civil liberties is horrifying. Abuses occur even though in every era, public-health officials always believe they're doing the right thing and acting in good faith".[8]

All serious policy makers are aware of the acute risk of handing over powers particularly to "good" people ("the road to Hell is paved with good intentions"). Victoria's public health law therefore expressly prohibits the exercise of arbitrary power: "actions ... should be proportionate to the public health risk sought to be prevented, minimised or controlled; and should not be made or taken in an arbitrary manner".[9]

---

[8] Efrati, Amir, "Public Safety v. Civil Liberties: Health Crisis Leads to New Case", *The Wall Street Journal*, 7 May 2009. Short URL: https://on.wsj.com/36ncFag.

[9] https://www.legislation.vic.gov.au/in-force/acts/public-health-and-wellbeing-act-2008/043.

But the excesses committed by public health practitioners in the past pale in comparison to the brutalities we have witnessed during this pandemic in the name of protecting us.

* * *

This debate is not just about deaths. It is about mass scale, society-wide torture. Lockdowns are a form of mass imprisonment and cause mental anguish on a mammoth scale.

When we imprison criminals, we give them food but exclude them from something vital: a normal life. During Victoria's lockdowns one person per family was permitted to go out to buy food. And so, like other prisoners in the jails of Australia, I did not go hungry. But is that all we live for – to get up, eat, and sleep?

How can anyone even begin to count the cost of isolation, of crushed plans, of lost happiness from not being able to undertake the myriads of mundane things we do? How can we even begin to count the cost of a life that is not allowed to be lived fully?

We live not just to avoid death. We have dreams. We have ambitions. Many of us work tirelessly for decades to build up a business. Some of us compose a picture. Others break into song. We smile at people in the park or when walking by to acknowledge them. We hug those who are in distress.

But these terrorist lockdowns have challenged our existence, our identity, our soul.

Our species has not been built, whether by God or by Nature, for such terror. I have no religion but I cannot even begin to imagine the anguish of those deprived of basic spiritual solace for over six months.

How does a government, our paid servant, most of whose employees have not a single creative bone in their body and who can never produce a cent's worth of value in a thousand lifetimes, get the right to destroy the work and dreams of those who do produce?

A lot of people with expertise in mental health have been writing to me. They want me to write about these harms which never show up in any GDP numbers.

Mental harms don't stop only with angst, anxiety or frustration. For some of us, things can break deep down within us. We all try to keep up appearances but, ultimately, we are a fragile species that needs social solace. I recall feeling like a zombie when my family had gone away to India for just a few weeks a few years ago. Loneliness kills. We should not at all be surprised to see additional suicides, domestic violence, child abuse and drug abuse incidents directly caused by the lockdowns. I hope anyone reading this will rather cry themselves to sleep than lose hope. Bear with me. We'll get there.

Despite the Victorian Government denying it, we are beginning to see signs of distress: "mental health support groups say they are being swamped with about a 20 per cent jump in pleas for help in Victoria since Melbourne's stage three and stage four lockdown restrictions began".[10] There has also been a significant increase in emergency room presentations for self-harm – which is a leading indicator of suicide. And Lifeline has recently had the most calls it has ever received on a single day.

* * *

Most tragic of all is that this whole episode never needed to happen. None of these witch doctor "remedies" (oppressions), none of this terror was part of our pandemic plans.

But for reasons that will surely require a Royal Commission to unearth, all pandemic plans – developing which must have cost taxpayers millions

---

[10] "Melbourne funeral company backs protest over surge in suicides", *Cairns News*, 20 September 2020. Short URL: https://bit.ly/2SgbgKp.

of dollars and which had been approved by scientists, lawyers and economists – were tossed out and a new-fangled lockdown experiment that no one had even considered previously, leave alone approve, was imposed in the blink of an eye.

On 24 June 2020 Sweden's State Epidemiologist Anders Tegnell exclaimed in astonishment: "It was as if the world had gone mad, and everything we had discussed was forgotten"[11]. Another medical professional, the Victorian Dr Eamonn Mathieson told Channel 9's Today show on 8 September 2020 that "[t]his attempt for viral elimination is irrational and unachievable. Simply it is madness and it needs to stop".[12]

But here's the thing. *No one* in leadership positions in society batted an eyelid or asked the simple question: "Why are we abandoning our well-though-out plans – which included a way to respond to even the worst-case pandemic – in order to rush into something that even a Grade 6 school child can say after five minutes of thinking, is harmful and dangerous?"

The state itself is broken – not just in Victoria, not just in Australia, but worldwide. This sorry episode is not just a case of broken governments. It is grand crime. Anything that is done on such a large scale in such an extreme, one-sided manner, with no regard to consequences, is no less than an act of terrorism. We will need a mechanism to bring the perpetrators to account.

All laws and international covenants have failed to stop these atrocities – except in Sweden, which has done an amazing job in protecting civil liberties, human dignity and the laws, even as it has done its best to focus

---

[11] Rolander, Niclas, "Sweden's Covid Expert Says 'World Went Mad' With Lockdowns", *Bloomberg Quint*, 24 June 2020. Short URL: https://bit.ly/3kQhGvZ.

[12] Oliveri, Natalie, "'It is madness': Doctors plead with Daniel Andrews to rethink virus response", *Today* show, Nine Now, 8 September 2020. Short URL: https://bit.ly/2HseUOV.

on the high-risk segment of its population. This Swedish exceptionalism and civilised approach is attributable at least in part to its Constitution which prohibits peacetime emergency powers. That is an essential learning for all Western societies that we will need to take forward.

In addition to not indulging in public health terrorism and mass-scale torture of its population, Sweden is the only nation that is likely therefore to emerge from this pandemic without an economic recession, after having just one negative quarter this year. All other nations – which imposed draconian lockdowns – are likely to end up with a sustained recession that could get significantly worse unless they change their policies right now.

For some inexplicable reason, much confusion prevails today about "Sweden's approach". That is only because our politicians, media and bureaucrats never bother to study anything in any detail (this also applies to their climate change policy). But to understand Sweden's approach is easy: just read Victoria's original plan – risk based, proportional, focused on flattening the curve, with community education and no mandatory masks. Sweden's approach is in our own plan if only we had opened it once.

* * *

It will probably take me a long time to regain trust in Victoria's police and politicians. I used to praise Victoria's police, marvelling at the high levels of trust and camaraderie between them and the people. Victoria Police had a band which performed in the CBD. I won't be going anywhere near it again. It would represent intolerable hypocrisy for the band to sing jolly songs after having smashed our fellow-citizen's head with a boot for not wearing a mask. I will now likely see Victoria Police officials as fundamentally evil till the end of my life. Or maybe I will change my mind in the future when this darkness and foreboding I feel around me finally goes – but at this point there is a trust deficit.

The politicians on all sides of politics who allowed this situation to arise and continue are equally marked. I no longer trust my public representatives who failed to do the *one* thing we pay them to do: to use their head on our behalf and ask hard questions.

I will now discuss some other big ticket issues in this chapter before moving to the details.

1.1 Comparing this pandemic with other pandemics. And what is its death rate?

The Victorian Chief Health Officer Brett Sutton is reported to have said in July 2020 that he considers this pandemic to be the "greatest public health challenge since the Spanish flu".[13]

Such a statement would have been accurate in mid-March 2020 when so much was still uncertain, but from mid-April scientists and policymakers of even a basic calibre could have readily deduced that this was no Spanish flu.

By mid-April almost all epidemiological models had been found to have wildly over-estimated likely deaths. For example, models reportedly based on Neil Ferguson's work had suggested that over 95,000 would die in Sweden without lockdowns.[14] To date 5,893 have died.

Regardless, now, in early October 2020, the following facts – which can be readily ascertained[15] – can help us to confidently assert that this is no

---

[13] Carey, Adam, and Webb, Carolyn, "Remote-learning move not enough to quell teachers' virus fears", *The Age*, 12 July 2020. Short URL: https://bit.ly/309l4tX.

[14] Miltimore, Jon, "Sweden's Actual COVID-19 Results Compared to What Modelers Predicted in April", Foundation for Economic Freedom, 28 July 2020. Short URL: https://bit.ly/3inEJMK.

[15] Sabhlok, Sanjeev, "Source of the data that I'm using to estimate scaled up pandemic deaths today for Spanish, Asian and Hong Kong flu", Sanjeev Sabhlok's blog, 30 September 2020. Short URL: https://bit.ly/2HA6V2i.

Spanish flu.

- The ordinary seasonal flu kills up to 0.65 million people worldwide each year – despite vaccines.

- Scaled up to today's population, the Hong Kong flu (1969) would kill 2.1 million people this year.

- Scaled up to today's population, the Asian flu (1957) would kill 4.6 million people this year.

- Scaled up to today's population, the Spanish flu (1918) would kill 210 million people over two years.

- Around 60 million people die in an average year worldwide of all causes.

- COVID-19 has killed 1 million to date.

Each of these data points requires some technical clarification but these figures are in the right ballpark.[16]

So how scared should we be – now?

The Spanish flu killed at least 50 million people worldwide in 1918 when the global population was 1.8 billion.[17] Proportionately, to be as lethal as the Spanish flu, today a virus would need to kill at least 210 million people. To date around one million have died from COVID-19. Compare this also with the 60 million who ordinarily die each year from all causes

---

[16] For instance, the data on the seasonal flu that I cite is the CDC's upper-end estimate. It seems fair to me to use the upper end estimate since the data on COVID-19 is likely to be somewhat inflated because it does not limit itself to deaths directly *caused* by this virus. On the other hand, data from countries like India is likely to include some under-reporting.

[17] Centers for Disease Control and Prevention, "1918 Pandemic (H1N1 virus)", website as at 2 October 2020. Short URL: https://bit.ly/2S7GraC.

worldwide. We have had *less than a week* (0.86 of a week) of additional deaths this year from COVID-19.

We can look at this in many ways. Let's work out the **population fatality rate**.

A simple calculation ((50/1800) x 1000) tells us that Spanish flu killed around 28 out of every 1,000 people over two years. 972 out of 1000 survived. That was good enough for the world to go on without any major hiccups. No lockdowns. No beatings by the police.

Today the world's population is 7.594 billion (7,594 million). One million have died to date from COVID-19. That means 0.13 out of every 1000 persons has died so far from COVID-19 ((1/7594) x 1000). This also means that 999.87 people have so far escaped death from COVID-19 out of every 1000.

Another, more manageable way to think about this, is that 99,987 persons have so far escaped death from COVID-19 out of every 100,000. Most of these 13 out of 100,000 who died were extremely old – but our governments did not bother much to protect them even though they could have.

What if this pandemic is more like the other two, non-Spanish flu, pandemics?

- Assume that this pandemic will end up in the range of the Hong Kong flu (and therefore may kill 2.1 million in the end) – then 0.28 persons will die out of every 1000, globally. In other words, 999.72 of us out of every 1000 will survive.

- Or assume that this will end up in the rage of the Asian flu. Then 4.6 million people worldwide may die, or 0.6 out of every 1000. In that case 999.4 persons will survive out of every 1000.

People who want to remain scared no matter what, tell us that this pandemic has not yet ended. And that may well be the case, although many scientists like Sunetra Gupta and Peter Doshi are telling us that this pandemic is largely over in many parts of the world.

But let's assume for a moment that this pandemic is not over. Let's assume there will be a second wave. If so, how big can it get?

We know for sure that there has never been a second or third pandemic wave in recorded history that is *hundreds* of times bigger than the first – but that (hundreds of times larger) is what it would take for this virus to be considered as lethal as Spanish flu. That doesn't make sense. Why would nature be so capricious?

If someone genuinely believes there will be a second wave that is hundreds of times bigger, they remain free to lock themselves indoors forever, waiting for it to come. All that the rest of us politely ask of them is that they not force us to be locked up as well, at the point of a gun.

There have been nine influenza pandemics during the past 300 years.[18] While there is no cyclicality about them, we average around one pandemic every 30 to 35 years. Some happen in quick succession, like the 1957 Asian flu and the 1969 Hong Kong flu. Others occur after a gap, like COVID-19 – our first major respiratory pandemic in 52 years.

This is why I call this pandemic a 1 in 30-year event. It sure is a nasty piece of work. But it is not enough to shut down the world. In fact, no matter how big a flu-like pandemic, it is *never* big enough to shut down the world.

Now, we might have been particularly alarmed if this virus was killing our young, like the Spanish flu did. But this virus almost entirely spares our children. We are blessed that our generation did not have to face a

---

[18] In 1729, 1732, 1781, 1830, 1833, 1889, 1918, 1957 and 1968.

pandemic on the scale of Spanish flu.

Let's shrug off our fears and get some sun on our face.

1.2 Important facts about the pandemic in Australia and Victoria

Let's get to our local issues for a moment.

Australia

Australia has a population of 26 million. Every day around 440 of us die during an average year, about 160,000 for the full year. As at 27 September 2020, 870 people had died in Australia allegedly from COVID-19.

Why "allegedly"?

That is because *The Age* reported on 10 September 2020[19] that "under federal Health Department guidelines, a death is defined for surveillance purposes as COVID-19-related if the person dies with the virus and there is no clear alternative cause of death, such as trauma. Those guidelines also stipulate that when a coroner's report finds a different cause of death, those findings take precedence". There are therefore likely to be at least a few COVID-19 reported deaths which did not happen "from" COVID-19 but "with" COVID-19.

Unreliable reporting is a significant issue in the USA and the UK, as well. Many doctors have reported on social media that some of those who are being currently listed as having died "with" COVID-19 never experienced any respiratory symptoms.

---

[19] Baker, Richard, "'Youngest COVID-19 victim may have died of another cause", *The Age*, 10 September 2020. Short URL: https://bit.ly/346a8yc.

We know that COVID-19 tests are problematic, which means no one can really be sure whether a person who supposedly "had" COVID-19 actually had it. Even if a person who died did genuinely have the virus, it means little for analytical purposes unless the virus *caused* the death. The medical fraternity needs to assure experienced data crunchers like me that only those deaths are being attributed to COVID-19 that had displayed *aggressive* symptoms of the COVID-19 disease.

But even assuming that all reported COVID-19 have been genuinely caused by this virus, that would amount to just under two days of annual additional deaths in Australia, to date. Of these who died, we know that most were the frail elderly – at least some of whom might have succumbed to other health issues sometime soon. Is the medical fraternity capturing reliable data on this issue? We need rock-solid statistics in order to understand the magnitude of the problem.

Victoria

In Victoria, about 40,000 people die each year of all causes. That's about 110 a day, with a substantial proportion of these deaths taking place within our nursing homes. As at 27 September 2020, only five people below the age of 50 had died in Victoria out of 782 reported COVID-19 deaths. And even within the 50-plus age group, the risk has been disproportionately high for those over 70 (729 of the 782 deaths were in this age group).

Clearly the elderly needed to have been protected. But were not.

What about ICU capacity? Victoria has "695 intensive care beds and the capacity to rapidly expand that number if cases surge, according to the state Health Minister Jenny Mikakos".[20] I believe that our ICUs were

---

[20] Mannix, Liam et.al., "What is Victoria's ICU capacity, and could we exceed it?", *The Age*, 17 July 2020. Short URL: https://bit.ly/3mTWsyR.

never even close to capacity. As of 4 September 2020, there were only 20 COVID-19 patients in ICUs.[21]

What started (correctly) as a strategy to "flatten the curve" to take the pressure off the health system converted somewhere on the way, without anyone of us being told, into a strategy of extreme suppression.

1.3 The Victorian Government abandoned its pandemic plan the moment things heated up

Pandemics are not an unexpected emergency. They can be, and are, fully anticipated. It is possible to contemplate all scenarios and prepare for them in advance. We know this because Sweden has managed this pandemic without the slightest panic and without brutalising its people. The Swedes were provided with relevant information and they chose their preventative actions voluntarily. No police were used against the people during the pandemic. The Swedes were offered reassurance, comfort, hope and faith that things will work out well. They are a decent people, a decent country.

Australia too had its plans.

Victoria's plan, called the *COVID-19 Pandemic plan for the Victorian Health Sector* was published on 10 March 2020.[22] It stated (correctly) that "COVID-19 is assessed as being of moderate clinical severity". But the plan did not limit itself only to a pandemic of moderate severity. It stated that "we are preparing so that we are ready to respond if a larger, or more severe outbreak occurs".

The plan was good. Based on a quick scan, I'd rate it 8 out of 10.

---

[21] Victorian Government, "Coronavirus update for Victoria - 04 September 2020", DHHS website. Short URL: https://bit.ly/34hD1I7.

[22] Victorian Government, "COVID-19 Pandemic Plan for the Victorian Health Sector", 10 March 2020. Short URL: https://bit.ly/2FPeqSJ.

It took a risk-based approach and "focused on protecting vulnerable Victorians". It explained that "older Victorians and people with chronic diseases are known to be at greater risk of COVID-19 infection". And it said that it would "ramp up risk reduction activity [for] at-risk groups".

The plan also included the most important principle of all – of proportionality: to "ensure a proportionate and equitable response". It wanted things to be "flexible and proportionate" and to "reduce [not eliminate] the morbidity and mortality associated with COVID-19". It thus spoke only about flattening of the curve, not about extreme suppression that borders on elimination – which is specifically forbidden by biosecurity law.

And the plan did not say that Victoria would be converted into a city-wide prison (that too with a ring of steel) while we waited for a vaccine to get invented, tested, approved, mass-produced and punched into every Victorian. The following, rather innovative, measures were not listed:

- imprison Victorians 23 hours a day within a radius of 5 kilometres because it is proven by science that respiratory viruses get particularly dangerous after 5 kilometres;

- of these 23 hours, no one must step out even one metre from their home for 9 hours (from 8 pm to 5 am) because respiratory viruses are well-known for their capacity to jump vast distances at night when they are able to go straight into people's nose;

- force people to wear a mask outdoors because the virus is well-known to have wings; and

- shut down hundreds of thousands of businesses since we have the power to borrow hundreds of billions of dollars – or, if required, get the Australian government to print money from thin air – to pay those whom we force to stay at home.

In other words, the 10 March 2020 Victorian was a well-balanced response to what was always going to be a difficult problem.

One might have perhaps inquired about its "workplace closures" strategy. But any concerns one may have had about this matter would have been alleviated because the plan also had the principles of risk and proportionality. As well, the *Public Health and Wellbeing Act 2008* imposes powerful restrictions on the powers of the Chief Health Officer to close workplaces. Any closures under Victoria's original pandemic plan would therefore have been extremely rare and well-targeted, not indiscriminate.

On 10 March 2020[23], Daniel Andrews stood up and outlined this plan to Victorians. He told us that there might be school closures, major event cancellations and working from home. But Andrews did not give the slightest hint of the rather big sledgehammer he was to later pull out from somewhere, maybe his garden shed. (In my *Australian Financial Review* piece,[24] I likened lockdowns to a sledgehammer being used to kill a swarm of mosquitoes.)

I have recently also sighted a 2014 news report that outlined the City of Melbourne's plan for dealing with a Spanish flu-type pandemic.[25] That too was a sensible plan. It did not mention society-wide lockdowns, curfews and mandatory masks outdoors. Professor Collignon is cited in that news report as saying that while cancelling big events might be appropriate in some cases, the authorities would have to consider both

---

[23] Urban, Rebecca, "Get ready for school closures, major event cancellations: Andrews", *The Australian*, 11 March 2020. Short URL: https://bit.ly/2G2235n.

[24] Sabhlok, Sanjeev, "Why I quit rather than be silenced: Vic Treasury insider", *Australian Financial Review*, 16 September 2020. Short URL: https://bit.ly/3jhUw0Z.

[25] Dow, Aisha, "Deadly flu pandemic could shut down Melbourne", *The Age*, 24 October 2020. Short URL: https://bit.ly/3cspctY.

the virus's severity and its likelihood of spreading, so in some cases there might be no need even to cancel a football match.

The AFL Grand Final would never have left Victoria had Daniel Andrews followed his pandemic plan.

1.4 The deaths of the elderly in Victoria that lockdowns failed to prevent

The data has been clear from the beginning that the aged and frail, and the immune-system compromised, are at far greater risk of succumbing to COVID-19.

Victoria's pandemic plan was about focusing where the risk is. But untargeted lockdowns allowed the virus to wreak havoc since the government took its eye off the ball. Eighty per cent of the government's effort went in "controlling" the broader society instead of focusing on aged care homes. As I will keep repeating throughout this book so no one forgets: many elderly deaths we have had could have been averted if the original pandemic plan had been followed.

It seems the virus crept into aged care homes which were not adequately barricaded against the virus. There are also unverified mumblings on social media that trained staff and even PPE were rationed and age care staff were circulating through multiple sites. There is chatter about infected patients having been transferred from hospitals into aged care facilities.

It is for a future Royal Commission to ask why we squandered billions of dollars to pay those whose jobs we forcibly took away, but were unable to find money to protect our elderly.

1.5 Government terrorism: Havoc, and potentially millions of deaths from lockdowns

Only one term fits the lockdowns: public health terrorism. These, below, are a few examples. The numbers are mind-boggling, leaving the 1 million deaths from COVID-19 far behind in their wake.

Children desperate and harming themselves, suicides

In the UK child suicides increased even in the early weeks of the lockdown. Domestic-abuse hotline calls were up over 60% in the U.K. Domestic-abuse murders of women increased significantly, possibly doubled, during lockdown. Drug abuse and alcoholism are up.[26] It is also likely that many families have been disrupted and divorces may have increased.

In Victoria, "Department of Health and Human Services data shows Victoria has recorded a 33 per cent rise in children presenting to hospital with self-harm injuries over the past six weeks, compared to a year earlier".[27]

Tens of thousands of additional deaths just in the UK and Australia

A report notes that "Pandemic shutdown 'means thousands more bowel cancer deaths'" in Australia.[28] In the UK, a report has stated: "The Health Data Research Hub for Cancer, who used health data to predict that there could potentially be an additional 18,000 additional deaths in

---

[26] Carter, Michael P., "Counting the Cost of U.K., U.S. Lockdowns", Letters, *Wall Street Journal*, 30 August 2020. Short URL: https://on.wsj.com/3kQexvT.

[27] Clayton, Rachel, "Statistics show increase in children presenting to hospitals after self-harming", ABC News, 8 August 2020. Short URL: https://ab.co/349vjzy.

[28] Scholefield, Antony, "Pandemic shutdown 'means thousands more bowel cancer deaths'", AusDoc, 21 September 2020. Short URL: https://bit.ly/342v2OP.

people with cancer, as a result of the pandemic".[29]

Patients are dying at home because, in sheer terror, they are not seeking urgent care. "Patients dying at home from causes other than Covid-19 are fuelling excess deaths across the UK. The data from the Office for National Statistics shows more than 6,700 extra deaths in homes across the UK in the past two months."[30]

Australia is reporting additional cancer deaths as well.[31]

Millions of people in developing countries will die from increased poverty, lack of medical care, atrocities and suicides

On 26 September 2020, the *Economist* magazine reported the World Bank's research that due to the lockdowns the number of extremely poor people (those who earn less than $1.90 a day) will rise by 70 to 100 million this year.[32] All economists know that poverty dramatically reduces the lifespan. Of these additional 100 million poor, it is not unreasonable to expect millions to lose far more years of life than all the years of life lost to COVID-19 to date.

Likewise, based on analysis by his organisation, the German Minister of Economic Cooperation and Development, Gerd Muller has said on 25 September 2020[33] that lockdowns have resulted in "one of the

---

[29] Health Data Research UK, "The Big C isn't COVID-19 - it's cancer", 25 August 2020. Short URL: https://bit.ly/3kSs8mxw.

[30] Donnelly, Laura, "Non-virus deaths at home behind surge in excess fatalities, figures show", *The Telegraph*, 2 September 2020. Short URL: https://bit.ly/3l92J8t.

[31] Scholefield, Antony, "Pandemic shutdown 'means thousands more bowel cancer deaths'", AusDoc, 21 September 2020. Short URL: https://bit.ly/342v2OP.

[32] *The Economist*, "Covid-19 has reversed years of gains in the war on poverty", 26 September 2020. Short URL: https://econ.st/3kSij84.

[33] Durden, Tyler, "German Minister Admits Lockdown Will Kill More Than COVID-19 Does", Zerohedge.com website, 26 September 2020. Short URL: https://bit.ly/2FXcgk2.

biggest" hunger and poverty crises in history. He believes that "an additional 400,000 deaths from malaria and HIV" will occur this year "on the African continent alone". Further, "half a million more will die from tuberculosis." This is largely attributable to the breakdown of food and medication supplies and lack of funding of the West's aid programs.

I should add that in India thousands of migrants were displaced by Modi's lockdowns and forced to walk home for hundreds of kilometres with family and children, without any support from government (they were treated like lepers on the way and often beaten up). Hundreds are reported to have died.

But that pales in comparison with increased suicides. India has around 230,000 suicides each year. Based only on limited data (for the district of Noida) I recently estimated that India could end up with an additional 50,000 suicides from lockdowns.[34]

It is not just in developing countries. We knkow that long-term unemployment can precipitate a vast number of mental health, family stability and health issues – including morbidity and mortality. These numbers will start flowing in from various surveys in the coming months.

Mothers are dying, foetuses are stillborn, children are dying or not even being conceived
The UNICEF has warned that disruptions arising from lockdowns could result in potentially devastating increases in maternal and child deaths.[35] And a Lancet study has reported a 50% increase in stillbirths

---

[34] Sabhlok, Sanjeev, Tweet of 8 September 2020. Short URL: https://bit.ly/3mXuVg0.
[35] UNICEF Press Release, 12 May 2020. Short URL: https://uni.cf/2GwOpHE.

during lockdowns in developing countries because of insufficient medical care.[36]

Moreover, the loss of economic stability in a household will make poor parents put off having children. How do we even begin to value the loss of a life the very conception of which we have disallowed?

Domestic abuse murders

These have possibly doubled: "According to Dame Vera Baird, victims' commissioner in the U.K., domestic-abuse murders of women increased significantly, possibly doubled, during lockdown".[37]

Elimination strategy to cost $320 billion just in Australia

On 29 September 2020 the Institute of Public Affairs found the "cost of trying to eliminate the coronavirus from Australia is more than annual government spending on defence, education, health and social security combined". "From June this year to the middle of 2022, the 'elimination strategy' being pursued by state and federal governments will cost $319bn, equivalent to 23 per cent of GDP, according to the report, Medical Capacity: An Alternative to Lockdowns".[38]

A grievous blow for the poor across the world

It is mainly the poor who are impacted by extended lockdowns. The rich are able to work from home. The lockdowns will unravel the lives

---

[36] Watson, Clare, "Stillbirth rate rises dramatically during pandemic", *Nature*, 15 September 2020. Short URL: https://on.wsj.com/3kQexvT.

[37] Grierson, Jamie, "Domestic abuse killings 'more than double' amid Covid-19 lockdown", *The Guardian*, 14 April 2020. Short URL: https://bit.ly/3ionpat.

[38] Creighton, Adam, "Coronavirus: Elimination strategy 'will cost us $319bn'", *The Australian*, 29 September 2020. Short URL: https://bit.ly/2ELCrcP.

of millions of poorer families and entrench social disadvantage for generations to come. Further, the lockdowns have choked off government revenues, forcing governments to borrow at a scale that is barely imaginable. In addition, governments are having to support those whose businesses they have forcibly stopped. This dual hit on government budgets will end up with decades of reduced services, with the poor facing the brunt.

Entrepreneurs hammered: a lifetime's work destroyed

Lost output is not just a matter of numbers. Some business owners in Victoria have contacted me to tell me of the colossal harms these lockdowns have caused to their lifetime's work. And business bankruptcies are not a matter only of financial loss but they disrupt families and can impact self-belief.

It is hard to know where to even begin. Who is going to be held to account for this devastation?

2
Other problems with lockdowns

> *Gauden Galea, the WHO's representative in China on 24 January 2020: "trying to contain a city of 11 million people is new to science. The lockdown of 11 million people is unprecedented in public health history, so it is certainly not a recommendation the WHO has made".*

Had our politicians *actually* "followed the science" lockdowns could never have happened. Or had they done a moral algebra – a simple tabulation of costs and benefits – then, too, the lockdowns could never have happened.

2.1 Lockdowns are not recommended by the W.H.O. "in any circumstances"

Stefan Baral, MD, Associate Professor and Infectious Disease Epidemiologist at John Hopkins School of Public Health tweeted on 16 August 2020: "I spent a decade in public health training and do not remember the lockdown lecture. At best, they drive inequities across socioeconomic lines. At worst, the same but no PH [public health] impact". And he cited four journal articles to prove his case.[39]

Scientists at the helm of pandemic management must have known (else they were not fit for that role) that there is not a single peer-reviewed paper before 2020 that recommends lockdowns. Instead, the literature regards lockdowns to be a public menace.

A 2006 paper rejected "large-scale quarantine" (lockdowns) which it said "should be *eliminated* from serious consideration" as a public health measure.

> There are no historical observations or scientific studies that support the confinement by quarantine of groups of possibly infected people for extended periods to slow the spread of influenza. A World Health Organization Writing Group, after reviewing the literature and considering contemporary international experience, concluded that "forced isolation and quarantine are ineffective and impractical." Despite this recommendation by experts, mandatory large-scale quarantine continues to be considered as an option by some authorities and government officials.
>
> The interest in quarantine reflects the views and conditions prevalent more than 50 years ago, when much less was known about the epidemiology of infectious diseases and when there was far less international and domestic travel in a less densely populated world. It is difficult to identify circumstances in the past half-century when large-scale quarantine has been effectively used in the control of any disease. The negative consequences of large-scale quarantine are so extreme (forced confinement of sick people with the well; complete

---

[39] Baral, Stefan. Tweet, 16 August 2020. Short URL: https://bit.ly/33XKHin.

restriction of movement of large populations; difficulty in getting critical supplies, medicines, and food to people inside the quarantine zone) that **this mitigation measure should be eliminated from serious consideration**.[40] (emphasis mine.)

The final nail on the coffin of those who argue that they have "followed the science" is the WHO's October 2019 report, "Non-pharmaceutical public health measures for mitigating the risk and impact of epidemic and pandemic influenza".[41] This report recommends face masks and some internal travel restrictions for major pandemics but prohibits lockdowns. On page three it states that contact tracing and quarantine of exposed individuals is **"not recommended in any circumstances"**.

At the beginning of the Wuhan lockdowns, Gauden Galea, the WHO's representative in China made it very clear on 24 January 2020 that: "trying to contain a city of 11 million people is new to science. The lockdown of 11 million people is unprecedented in public health history, so it is certainly **not a recommendation** the WHO has made."[42]

To understand the meaning of this recommendation we need to read the associated annexure to the WHO report ("Annex: Report of systematic literature reviews" (chapter 3. Social distancing measures)).

Among its supporting documents is a 2004 paper, "Factors That Make

---

[40] Inglesby, Thomas V., et. al., "Disease Mitigation Measures in the Control of Pandemic Influenza", *Biosecurity and Bioterrorism*. Volume 4, Number 4, 2006. Short URL: https://bit.ly/3mTUrCN.

[41] World Health Organisation, "Non-pharmaceutical public health measures for mitigating the risk and impact of epidemic and pandemic influenza", October 2019. Short URL: https://bit.ly/3mPsmg0.

[42] Senger, Michael P., "China's Global Lockdown Propaganda Campaign", *Tablet*, 16 September 2020. Short URL: https://bit.ly/2RXS0RA.

an Infectious Disease Outbreak Controllable"[43], by C. Fraser, S. Riley, RM Anderson, and NM Ferguson (the same Neil Ferguson we have encountered earlier). The papers states:

> for SARS, our analysis indicates that effective isolation of symptomatic patients is sufficient to control an outbreak. Influenza, on the other hand, is predicted to be **very difficult to control even with 90% quarantining and contact tracing** because of the high level of presymptomatic transmission. (emphasis mine.)

Note this paper is not only vigorously against mass-scale quarantines, it is also against mass-scale contact tracing (and testing). This conclusion also passes the pub test: How is it even possible to keep a virus permanently under lock and key if it is able to transmit even when it is asymptomatic or mildly symptomatic?

That the science is vigorously against lockdowns was re-confirmed in a recent cross-country study which showed that "full lockdowns, border closures, and high rate of COVID-19 testing were not associated with reduced number of critical cases or overall mortality".[44]

The summary of "lockdown science" is best provided by Harvard Medical School Professor Martin Kulldorff (who has been supportive of my work for the past many months): By increasing other types of morbidity during lockdowns, we end up with much higher mortality in the long-term with lockdowns.[45]

---

[43] Fraser, Christophe et.al., "Factors that make an infectious disease outbreak controllable", *PNAS*, 20 April 2004. Short URL: https://bit.ly/341gRcF.

[44] Chaudhry, Rabail et. al., "A country level analysis measuring the impact of government actions, country preparedness and socioeconomic factors on COVID-19 mortality and related health outcomes", *EClinical Medicine*, 21 July 2020. Short URL: https://bit.ly/3j2gMf7.

[45] Kulldorff, Martin, Tweet, 29 August 2020. Short URL: https://bit.ly/2RUc0oe.

2.2 Lockdowns breach many international covenants

Let me summarise a few of the covenants that have been breached by governments.

1) Nuremberg Code

The reason Victoria's 10 March 2020 pandemic plan did not include lockdowns and mandatory masks outdoors is because both these have been comprehensively rejected by science. Therefore, this much is certain: that *under no circumstances are lockdowns a science*. They are, at best, a science experiment.

So, let's say that some hare-brained "scientist" wanted to try a lockdown experiment. He would need ethics approval for his experiment. What is the chance of his getting such approval? None. Lockdowns comprehensively violate the Nuremberg Code which protects human subjects of experiments from cruelty.[46]

According to the Code, a human experiment must meet these conditions:

1) Voluntary consent is essential.
2) The results of any experiment must be for the greater good of society.
3) Human experiments should be based on previous animal experimentation.
4) Experiments should be conducted by avoiding physical/mental suffering and injury.
5) No experiments should be conducted if it is believed to

---

[46] Jarmusik, Natalie, "The Nuremberg Code and its impact on clinical research", IMARC Research, 9 April 2019. Short URL: https://bit.ly/2HxBd5Y.

cause death/disability.

6) The risks should never exceed the benefits.

7) Adequate facilities should be used to protect subjects.

8) Experiments should be conducted only by qualified scientists.

9) Subjects should be able to end their participation at any time.

10) The scientist in charge must be prepared to terminate the experiment when injury, disability, or death is likely to occur.

Lockdowns are almost certain to be a prosecutable offence under international law.

2) Universal Declaration on Bioethics and Human Rights

Article 6 of the Universal Declaration on Bioethics and Human Rights states:

> Any preventive, diagnostic and therapeutic medical intervention is only to be carried out with the **prior, free and informed consent** of the person concerned, based on adequate information. The consent should, where appropriate, be expressed and may be withdrawn by the person concerned at any time and for any reason without disadvantage or prejudice. (emphasis mine.)

Lockdowns presumably come under the category of a "preventative health" intervention. If that is so, then they require prior informed consent from *each individual*, i.e. each one of us. No one took my consent.

3) WHO International Health Regulations 2005

The International Health Regulations 2005 specify that "a health measure does not include law enforcement or security measures". To me this means (or at least the spirit of the regulation means) that police must not be used to enforce public health measures.

But not only did Daniel Andrews use Victoria's police indiscriminately, he recently passed a Bill in the Lower House of the Victorian Parliament which threatens to give police powers even to those who have not been trained for it. One hopes that this Bill will be disallowed by Victoria's Upper House.

2.3. Does a moral (prudential) algebra or a cost-benefit test of lockdowns tell us something different?

Is there some other to justify lockdowns? Would a cost-benefit test help?

A moral or prudential algebra

Benjamin Franklin's "prudential algebra", outlined in a letter he wrote to the chemist Joseph Priestly in 1772[47], is the simplest way to think about the trade-offs involved in our daily life.

> [M]y Way is, to divide half a Sheet of Paper by a Line into two Columns, writing over the one Pro, and over the other Con.
>
> Then during three or four Days Consideration I put down under the different Heads short Hints of the different Motives that at different Times occur to me for or against the Measure. When I have thus got them all together in one View,

---

[47] Founders Online. Short URL: https://bit.ly/3js3AAE

I endeavour to estimate their respective Weights; and where I find two, one on each side, that seem equal, I strike them both out: If I find a Reason pro equal to some two Reasons con, I strike out the three. If I judge some two Reasons con equal to some three Reasons pro, I strike out the five; and thus proceeding I find at length where the Ballance lies; and if after a Day or two of farther Consideration nothing new that is of Importance occurs on either side, I come to a Determination accordingly.

And tho' the Weight of Reasons cannot be taken with the Precision of Algebraic Quantities, yet when each is thus considered separately and comparatively, and the whole lies before me, I think I can judge better, and am less likely to take a rash Step; and in fact I have found great Advantage from this kind of Equation, in what may be called Moral or Prudential Algebra.

Obviously, such thinking is even more important when making a decision that can affect the lives of millions of people. We cannot avoid the analysis of pros and cons, and weights. Even a one-page tabulation of these pros and cons of lockdowns would tell us that they can never be justified.

The standard cost benefit test is for matters in which government does not take extra lives

In the normal course of policy making, a government intervenes in the market to try to resolve its failures. To assist decision making, we use cost-benefit analysis (CBA) which is the practical implementation of Bentham's utilitarianism – the greatest good of the greatest number.

Consider town planning. In this case we compare the loss of utility to some people from (say), a tall building in their neighbourhood with the financial cost imposed on society by limiting the height of a building. These are ultimately financial calculations of some sort.

In more challenging cases, we might compare financial costs and the "statistical value" of a life. For example, in the field of occupational health and safety, the government imposes (financial) costs on businesses to undertake measures to prevent the loss of life at work. But we probably should not impose a cost of $100 million on the business sector in order to save one life. Instead, we could perhaps impose a cost of up to maybe $5 million or whatever the "statistical value of life" is currently estimated to be.

The standard cost benefit test for matters in which government actively *takes* **extra lives**

The Benthamite principle might probably still apply when a government actively takes extra lives in order to prevent the loss of other lives. There is a robust literature on how this could be done.

On 13 August 2020 the eminent philosopher Peter Singer, the Laureate Professor at the Centre for Applied Philosophy and Public Ethics at the University of Melbourne is reported to have expressed his surprise that governments had taken such strong actions without presenting cost benefit analyses.[48]

Peter Singer said that when doing a cost benefit analysis of lockdowns we must take into account the number of years of life lost, not just the number of deaths: "That it's less tragic for a 90-year-old to die than a 30-year-old seems clear to me". We must reject outright the virtue-sig-

---

[48] Creighton, Adam, "Lockdowns could eventually be seen as an over-reaction, says philosopher Peter Singer", *The Australian*, 13 August 2020. Short URL: https://bit.ly/337i6rK.

nalling approach of health professionals like Devi Sridhar who insist on valuing all lives equally.[49]

He noted that it is "totally reasonable" for governments to assign a value to human life for the purposes of allocating public spending. "Otherwise you get irrational decisions where the department of road safety spends $8m to save a life whereas you could save $4m in another area".

The University of Melbourne Vice-Chancellor Duncan Maskell also said this the other day, that "decision-makers must consider the role of quality-adjusted life year (QALY), a unit of measurement used by economists to predict and assess the impact of health policies. In simple terms, it assumes that a life near its end, whether because of disease or advanced age, is empirically different to a healthy life closer to its beginning".[50]

Based on this logic, a number of independent scholars have attempted a cost-benefit test of lockdowns (including Gigi Foster and Bjørn Lomborg). In each case, lockdowns have been found to be uniformly bad, without any redeeming features.

But can we possibly compare lives taken by Nature with lives taken by Man (government)?

But there is a fundamental problem that we need think about when considering the relevance of a standard CBA for lockdowns.

Can we calculate the "benefit" of a crime? How can we calculate the value of life that governments actively destroy? Bentham probably never imagined a situation in which governments would actively destroy some citizens in order to achieve a "social optimum".

---

[49] Sridhar, Devi, Tweet, 5 April 2020. Short URL: https://bit.ly/3kORUbf.

[50] Le Grand, Chip, "Melbourne Uni chief says Victoria must address difficult ethical questions", *The Sydney Morning Herald*, 19 September 2020. Short URL: https://bit.ly/3kTEXwK.

In "normal" public health policy we impose costs on the business community (say, shutting down a restaurant which has cockroaches) in order to *save* some lives. But lockdowns don't just do that – they kill unspecified persons X, Y and Z (e.g. a young person who may commit suicide) in order to save the lives from COVID-19 of other unspecified persons A, B, and C. Coercive lockdowns are like a Trolley problem, not a comparison of utilities.[51] How can we compare the "total" happiness generated by an option (the greatest good of the greatest number) that kills thousands, possibly millions across the world?

I believe we might well be able to do a CBA as a first test of the lockdown policy but even if a CBA proves that lockdowns are justified, they are fundamentally immoral.

We must create an associated Crimes Register along with each CBA that lists the number of people the government will sacrifice at the altar of the Public Health God.

Is there a duration for which lockdowns might prove beneficial?

What about those who argue that lockdowns might work for a short duration? Professor Emanuel Ornelas suggested on 28 March 2020 that there might be a duration for which lockdowns might reduce overall costs.[52]

And Boris Johnson's pandemic adviser Graham Medley said on 4 April 2020[53] that, "for all countries at some point, prolonged lockdowns risk causing more suffering than the killer virus itself". This suggests Medley

---

[51] Wikipedia, Trolley Problem. Short URL: https://bit.ly/2Sa0RQf.
[52] Ornelas, Emanuel, "Managing economic lockdowns in an epidemic", VOX-EU, 28 March 2020. Short URL: https://bit.ly/30eIlKV.
[53] Dettmer, Jamie, "Officials Face Hard Questions in Weighing COVID Lockdown Exit Strategies", VOA News, 4 April 2020. Short URL: https://bit.ly/3idnhuF.

also thinks there might be a duration when lockdowns do not cause this additional suffering.

I reject these views because even if a CBA can tell us about such a duration, the idea of actively harming others to save some of us is morally abhorrent.

Further such views are inconsistent with the WHO's prohibition on lockdowns and with Professor Martin Kulldorffs' well-argued view that no duration of lockdowns is justifiable since by increasing other types of morbidity during lockdowns, we always end up with higher mortality in the long-term.

How about imposing lockdowns not at the beginning but at the end – when a vaccine is already at hand?

Even then I cannot how coercion can be justified. In a case like this, those who wish to take the vaccine (probably because of their higher risk profile – people like me) can "lockdown" themselves.

Voluntarism trumps coercive, untargeted lockdowns in all circumstances.

3

Inner workings of a viral pandemic

In this chapter I outline the elements of virus biology. My hope is to show that we are not helpless against COVID-19.

3.1. Viruses are a part of us
This virus that has taken the world by storm, SARS-CoV-2 (the disease it causes is called COVID-19), arose in China in around October 2019.

Viruses exist somewhere in between the world of the living and the nonliving. They arose quite early during the formation of life on earth.[54] It may come as a surprise to some of us, but we are built from virus genetic material. About 8 per cent of human genetic material comes

---

[54] Arnold, Carrie, "Could Giant Viruses Be the Origin of Life on Earth?", National Geographic, 17 July 2014. Short URL https://on.natgeo.com/3mPCmFY.

from a virus[55]: "the genomes of humans and other mammals contain DNA derived from the insertion of bornaviruses, RNA viruses whose replication and transcription takes place in the nucleus".

This viral toolkit that we inherit in our body's operations manual (DNA) we then pass on to our children perhaps to train their innate immune system.

The vast majority of "vaccines" are administered to us by Nature

The most significant risk to a prematurely born neonate sheltered in a bubble is that it can die from the mildest infection. That is also why the arrival of the Europeans so severely impacted native American and indigenous Australian populations, since they had no resistance to the novel bugs the Europeans were carrying.

It all begins with our children playing and interacting with Nature and with each other – a process during which they catch viruses and their immune system strengthens its already superb weaponry. This is how Nature vaccinates us from most of the bugs we will face, a process that has been going on for millions of years, well before any vaccines were invented. Without these natural vaccines, we might have needed to take a good number of vaccines each day of our life – given there are hundreds of thousands of viruses that can infect mammals.[56]

---

[55] University of Texas at Arlington, "Evolutionary surprise: Eight percent of human genetic material comes from a virus", *Science Daily*, 8 January 2010. Short URL: https://bit.ly/3i0VH3z.

[56] Virology blog, "How many viruses on Earth?", 6 September 2013. Short URL: https://bit.ly/3mPTOdE. It is estimated that 320,000 different viruses infect mammals.

3.2 How our body fights viruses

There are at least three stages to be crossed by a virus before it can fell us.

Stage 1: The viral load has to be sufficient

Viral load depends upon the strength of transmission (e.g. a sneeze and its "quantum"), proximity to us, duration of exposure, level of UV radiation (in summer the virus is rapidly destroyed by ultraviolet radiation), personal protection (e.g. gloves, glasses or masks), hygiene (handwashing), the nature of our occupation (farmers are less susceptible compared with those who interact with others a lot), culture (e.g. how we meet and greet each other), and so on.

In the ordinary course of interactions in an average society, transmitting sufficient viral load is relatively difficult. That is why few, if any, flu pandemics have managed to infect more than a quarter of the world's population. Most estimates for the Spanish flu are in the range of a quarter to a third of the world population getting infected.[57] Likewise, only around 24% of the world's population was ever infected by H1N1 (Swine flu).[58]

Some case studies of COVID-19 support a view that it, too, cannot possibly infect all of us – mainly due to low viral load. In the case of the cruise ship Diamond Princess and aircraft carrier Theodore Roosevelt, only around 20% of the residents were reportedly infected. That could be due to relatively sporadic inter-mingling between residents on different levels of the ship. But that also broadly mimics how societies, overall, actually interact, although much depends on the relevant culture and

---

[57] Centers for Disease Control and Prevention, "1918 Pandemic (H1N1 virus)", website as at 2 October 2020. Short URL: https://bit.ly/2S7GraC.

[58] Roos, Robert, "Study puts global 2009 pandemic H1N1 infection rate at 24%", Centre for Infectious Disease Research and Policy, University of Minnesota, 24 January 2013. Short URL: https://bit.ly/2EJaJ06.

density of living.

When density of living increases, the virus spreads more. At least 44 of 70 University of Texas at Austin students on a chartered plane to Mexico for spring break tested positive, as did 52 of 61 who attended a choir practice in Washington. Likewise, the spread of infection within prisons and in aged-care nursing homes is generally more than 20%.

Its high density might explain New York's higher rate of infection (and deaths). And also, why Alaska has seen 20 times fewer deaths per million than New York. If this analysis is correct, then this virus is likely spread less in regional Australia than in Melbourne's or Sydney's CBD.

Stage 2: The virus has to beat our innate immune system

Like a Swiss Army knife, our non-specific innate immune system is able to battle any new virus, usually with some success. Innate immunity is a pattern-recognition "skill" possessed by phagocytic cells (monocytes, macrophages, and neutrophils) and natural killer cells, among others.

When we battle a virus with our innate immunity, we generally do not show symptoms. Its operation can be compared with hand-to-hand guerrilla combat – unlike the adaptive immune system which is like a full-blown Seventh Fleet plus a B-29 Superfortress bomber squad that decimates both the virus and our infected cells.

Innate immunity is genetically transmitted (it perhaps has something to do with the 8% viral genetic material that we carry in our DNA) and varies among persons. Like other forms of immunity, it declines with age.

Does the human species have innate immunity for this novel coronavirus? A 21 April 2020 paper entitled, "Long-term Coexistence of SARS-CoV2) with Antibody Response in COVID-19 Patients" by Bin Wang et. al., noted that "without antibody-mediated adaptive immunity, innate immunity may still be powerful enough to eliminate SARS-CoV-2".

I suspect that our species' level of innate immunity to this virus is not too high. Had it been otherwise, we would not see the high levels of infection in choirs, prisons and nursing homes.

There is an interesting twist to this part of our immune system. It is possible to "train" it by administering a vaccine for a different bug. A 11 May 2020 paper entitled, "BCG-induced trained immunity: can it offer protection against COVID-19?" by Luke O'Neill and Mihai Netea suggests that our innate immune system could be "trained" via non-COVID19 vaccines like the BCG (anti-tuberculosis) vaccine. In countries where the BCG vaccine is widely administered, like in India, it seems to have played a role in protecting people from COVID-19.

Stage 3: Finally, the virus has to beat our adaptive immune system

This heavy-duty part of our system delivers the knock-out blow to the enemy. It is only activated after the innate system calls for help. Adaptive immune responses are based on T cells, B cells and antibodies.

Unfortunately, sometimes this system gets a bit overzealous and indiscriminate – killing not just the infected but healthy cells (through what is called a cytokine storm – a blitzkrieg). It seems that one way to prevent this system from getting too excited about the fight is to pour a lot of Vitamin D on it. This is standard science found in all textbooks.

In fact, there is a good evidence that Vitamin D helps with COVID-19: "Vitamin D cuts chance of coronavirus death by half".[59] It is puzzling why governments have not promoted this well-established fact to get the elderly, who often have insufficient Vitamin D, to take this Vitamin as

---

[59] Somerville, Ewan, "Vitamin D 'cuts chance of coronavirus death by half', study finds", *Evening Standard*, 27 September 2020. Short URL: https://bit.ly/36mWwBE.

well as Vitamin C and zinc? (I take these regularly: obviously the reader should consult their physician before doing the same.)

This part of our immune system produces the antibodies which can be tested by serological assays. The antibodies stay behind for some time in the body just in case a similar virus tries to stage a comeback. In most cases, antibodies fade with time.

Cross-reactivity

In some cases, fighting off an infection (say, common cold) primes our T cells and also apparently some antibody components, to fight other related infections (say, COVID-19). This process is called cross-reactivity and has turned out to be very important in helping to fight COVID-19.

This novel coronavirus is similar to the four existing ones (229E, HKU1, NL63, and OC43) that cause around 20% of the common colds. Research has concluded (in line with scientific expectations) that a recent infection from one of these four can protect us against COVID-19.[60] This cross-reactivity, in my opinion, at least partly explains the extremely low COVID-19 death toll in India – where just four days of additional annual deaths have been attributed to COVID-19 to date.

I share my own experience here. I used to catch the common cold frequently when I lived in India (mainly due to the low hygiene standards in that society) but I hardly ever get one in Australia. Since cross-reactivity does not last too long, perhaps in this case for only a few months or a

---

[60] A 23 July 2020 study entitled "Pre-existing and de novo humoral immunity to SARS-CoV-2 in humans" by Kevin W. Ng et. al. provides details. The study looked at 262 samples from SARS-CoV-2-uninfected adults and 48 SARS-CoV-2-uninfected children and adolescents in London. It found that at least 21 of the 48 children showed cross-reactivity (SARS-CoV-2 neutralising antibodies) from prior exposure to common cold coronaviruses, but only 6% of adults showed cross-reactivity.

couple of years, this means I am unlikely now to have retained the ability to fight COVID-19 from cross-reactivity. But the average Indian adult who keeps getting the common cold is likely to have a significantly higher capacity to fight COVID-19.

Even the elderly in India have not died in the large numbers initially anticipated. That's possibly because Indian grandparents often look after their grandchildren, which transfers the common cold virus to them, thus reinforcing their immune system.

3.3 A natural vaccine to COVID-19 is probably to be found in our kindergartens

I wasn't facetious when I put out a Tweet on 27 July 2020 to suggest that we "smear everyone's face with snot collected from pre-school children. That should vaccinate them against c19".

Gross, but that's broadly similar to what Edward Jenner did when he took the "stuff" from cowpox sores to protect people against smallpox. Of course, there's undoubtedly a better way: bottling live harmless coronavirus under controlled environments into a nasal spray. We should, however, not expect pharmaceutical companies to research and market such a thing any time soon: there's no money in it. And, of course, it will also face a lot of regulatory hurdles.

On 2 September 2020 Professor Sunetra Gupta who teaches theoretical epidemiology at Oxford University welcomed the re-opening of schools. She considers that children "would benefit from being exposed to this and other seasonal coronaviruses". She is basically saying the same thing: that getting a less harmful infection is good as it protects us against the more serious ones in the future. It is possible that in the future we might be pleased when our children catch this coronavirus, like we were once pleased when they caught chickenpox before the availability of an effective vaccine.

Many people have missed the significance of the good news about cross-reactivity amid the panic.

3.4 In sum, we humans are not defenceless against SARS-CoV-2

Professor Sunetra Gupta suggested in an interview with UnHerd on 21 May 2020 that humanity is likely to have robust innate and cross-reactive immunity to this virus.[61] To that we can add trained immunity from vaccines like BCG. This was clear even in May 2020 when the panic was at its peak. But no one listened to her.

This fact would have calmed down the panic but scientists at the helm did not listen to Gupta. In doing so they are following a well-treaded pattern. For, during the Swine flu pandemic as well, the same thing had happened. People discovered that humans already had strong immunity to it but after discovering this re-assuring fact, everyone forgot.

Derek Lowe noted in an article in *ScienceMag* on 15 May 2020, entitled, "Good News on the Human Immune Response to the Coronavirus", cross-reactivity was "a big factor in making the H1N1 flu epidemic less severe than had been initially feared – the population already had more of an immunological head start than thought".

Somehow, the scientists at the helm don't care to remember the lessons from previous pandemics. A 17 September 2020 paper by Peter Doshi in the *British Medical Journal*, entitled, "Covid-19: Do many people have pre-existing immunity?"[62] discusses how people have forgot the lessons

---

[61] Sayers, Freddie, "Sunetra Gupta: Covid-19 is on the way out", UnHerd, 21 May 2020. Short URL: https://bit.ly/3cLMZ8q.

[62] Doshi, Peter, "Covid-19: Do many people have pre-existing immunity?", BMJ, 17 September 2020. Short URL: https://bit.ly/33TO8GE.

from the swine flu pandemic.

> In late 2009, months after the World Health Organization declared the H1N1 "swine flu" virus to be a global pandemic, Alessandro Sette was part of a team working to explain why the so called "novel" virus did not seem to be causing more severe infections than seasonal flu.
>
> Their answer was pre-existing immunological responses in the adult population: B cells and, in particular, T cells, which "are known to blunt disease severity." Other studies came to the same conclusion: people with pre-existing reactive T cells had less severe H1N1 disease. In addition, a study carried out during the 2009 outbreak by the US Centers for Disease Control and Prevention reported that 33% of people over 60 years old had cross reactive antibodies to the 2009 H1N1 virus, leading the CDC to conclude that "some degree of pre-existing immunity" to the new H1N1 strains existed, especially among adults over age 60.
>
> The data forced a change in views at WHO and CDC, from an assumption before 2009 that most people "will have no immunity to the pandemic virus" to one that acknowledged that "the vulnerability of a population to a pandemic virus is related in part to the level of pre-existing immunity to the virus." But by 2020 it seems that lesson had been forgotten.

Doshi then shows that because of all these reasons, the herd immunity threshold is much lower than initially anticipated:

> While most experts have taken the R0 for SARS-CoV-2 (generally estimated to be between 2 and 3) and concluded that at least 50% of people need to be immune before herd immunity is reached, Gomes and colleagues calculate the

threshold at 10% to 20%". (R0 is the reproduction number.)

This analysis also suggests that the most destructive phase of the pandemic is largely over in parts of the world like Sweden and New York. But it is definitely not over in Australia where the virus has been excessively suppressed. Australia remains almost as susceptible as it was six months ago.

Professor Scott Atlas, who now advises the President of the USA on public health policy for the pandemic, assured the world on 23 September 2020 about the human immune system:

> [I]mmunity to the infection is not solely determined by the percent of people who have antibodies. If you look at the research – and there's been about 24 papers at least on the immunity from T-cells – that's a different type of immunity than antibodies. And ... according to the papers from Sweden, Singapore, and elsewhere there is cross-immunity. And the combination of those makes the antibodies a small fraction of the people that have immunity.[63]

We are not defenceless. When a novel virus enters our ecosystem most of us can fight it off. Our bodies have been "built" over hundreds of millions of years[64] of evolutionary battles with bugs.

And that is why after one full year of trying to attack human defences, the virus has managed to kill only one million of us, out of a 7,594 million strong force.

We are not all going to die from COVID-19. It is other things that will (ultimately) kill us.

---

[63] White House, "Remarks by President Trump in Press Briefing", 23 September 2020. Short URL: https://bit.ly/2SeyVuF.

[64] Hundreds of millions of years of prior evolutionary phases of life are incorporated into the human DNA.

3.5 Herd immunity now likely already exists or is very close in many countries

If a vaccine did not make the previous big respiratory pandemics go away, how did they end? A number of evolutionary and adaptive pressures tend to bring pandemics down to manageable levels.

The minor factors among these include:

- those amongst us with weaker immunity tend to die first, leaving those with stronger immunity behind; and
- the more lethal strains of the virus tend to die with host (the dead body of the person they kill), leaving the less lethal strains behind.

The main mechanism, however, is herd immunity.

When a large number of us manage to fight the virus successfully and boost our already robust natural defences (through new antibodies and the like), the virus finds nowhere to go. At that stage our species can be said to have successfully battled the virus as a "herd": we have herd immunity.

Herd immunity is not perfect. It does not mean the virus has been eradicated. And it does not mean that we have all magically become immune. All it means is that due to low viral load and higher levels of immunity in the population, further viral spread is greatly reduced and we can revert to a normal life.

Over time, most respiratory viruses degrade into a seasonal variety that might sporadically kill a few of us, particularly those with an immune system already weakened by age or some other disease.

The Nobel prize-winning scientist Michael Levitt was among the first (apart from a few others like Sunetra Gupta and John P. A. Ioannidis) to suggest that the herd immunity threshold for this novel coronavirus is much lower than was earlier thought. Professor Sunetra Gupta has long been arguing that there won't be a major second wave in cities and countries where the virus has killed around 0.1% of the population. I consider this figure might be more like 0.06% of the population (using Sweden as a benchmark).

Likewise, Mike Yeadon, a former Chief Science Officer for Pfizer for 16 years[65] recently co-authored a paper entitled "How Likely is a Second Wave?" A news report about the paper on 1 October 2020, notes: "Dr. Yeadon … argues that the threshold for herd immunity may be much lower than previously thought, and may have been reached in many countries already." And further, "there is no science to suggest a second wave should happen".

---

[65] Lopez, Ralph, "Former Chief Science Officer for Pfizer Says 'Second Wave' Faked on False-Positive COVID Tests, 'Pandemic is Over'", HubPages, 1 October 2020. Short URL: https://bit.ly/2RZZV0F.

4
The broken State

Men, it has been well said, think in herds; it will be seen that they go mad in herds, while they only recover their senses slowly, and one by one.

Charles Mackay

Australian governments, including in Victoria, abandoned their carefully crafted pandemic plans the moment the pandemic started. They gave into the Great Hysteria that was being stoked by the media. In this chapter I outline the events and issues that this breakdown of governance has raised in my mind.

And it not just the governments that have failed. The fuller apparatus of the state and most of society's institutions have cracked, if not broken.

4.1 Alarm bells in my head when lockdowns were imposed

For most of the past two decades that I've lived in Melbourne I have been quite satisfied with the way Victoria's governance system works. Over these two decades, I have spent 15 years at the Victorian Department of Treasury and Finance ("the Treasury") as an economist, advising the government of the day on regulatory and economic policy matters across areas such as agriculture, forestry, water, energy, town planning and local government.

While I was not personally involved with the development of Victoria's pandemic plan or public health measures to deal with this pandemic, I assumed that the policy principles followed in the ordinary course of affairs, such as a risk-based approach, proportionality and transparency – would be applied while designing the relevant plans and measures.

The Treasury is a collegiate organisation. Like all good organisations, it operates as a collaborative group of people working, in this case, to ensure the prosperity of all Victorians. It is my experience that officials within the Treasury do not hesitate (indeed, I would imagine that it is an expectation) to raise any concerns about any matter that may impact Victorians. These concerns are then fed to those better placed to act. It is this collegiate approach that makes Victoria's Treasury the best in Australia. (I would still say that, except for a few matters that I discuss in the last chapter.)

From late February 2020 onwards, I provided suggestions both verbally and in writing within the organisation on possible ways to manage this pandemic. My advice was based on my experience of risk management (that I gained during my stint at the Victorian WorkCover Authority) and of good regulatory processes. I recommended an age-based risk management approach. This approach was later confirmed by many senior scientists such as Martin Kulldorff. More importantly, I subsequently discovered that the Victorian Government's own pandemic plan of 10 March 2020 also advised this approach.

From 16 March 2020, a state of emergency came into effect in the State of Victoria and a few days later draconian lockdowns were introduced, of the kind imposed in Wuhan in China and across Italy. That sent alarm bells ringing in my head. These measures were a massive overreach, entirely unjustified from *any* regulatory policy or human rights perspective.

We do not elect a government to focus on a single risk. To the contrary, a government has an obligation to consider the welfare of the entire society – by considering not only all of the current impacts but likely future impacts of any policy option. In doing so the government has to balance all risks in society. It should not get obsessed with eliminating a particular risk.

The *Victorian Guide to Regulation* observes that "[i]t is not possible for governments to provide a completely 'risk-free' society, or to prevent every possible event that might cause harm". Further: "the direct and indirect costs imposed by regulatory approaches may not be … immediately obvious. Risk regulation that is poorly targeted or costly will divert resources from other priorities".

Accordingly, the Victorian Government needed, in February 2020, to commission a detailed analysis of alternative policy options that took into account scenarios, with and without a vaccine. After that, the Government should have chosen the best option, cognisant of the uncertainty and considering also the need to intrude in the least invasive way possible into human freedoms.

This analysis and the policies arising from it should then have been immediately published for public comment and updated as new information emerged (such as the fact that most epidemiological models used in March 2020 had exaggerated the risk posed by COVID-19).

But the lockdown screw got tighter and tighter. Just as comprehensive data started coming in from mid-April that this virus is *far* less lethal than originally thought, the Victorian Government started tightening the screw and has continued to do so, till now it has become truly intolerable to live in Melbourne. Not just home imprisonment: one cannot even breathe fresh oxygen. This is a comprehensive attack on one's existence.

I kept raising concerns within the Treasury but after not being taken seriously, I gave up.

Fortunately, I had another pathway to raise my concerns. For the past two decades I have had a life's mission: to reform India's governance system. As part of this mission, I have written many newspaper articles including centre-pieces in *Times of India*, the world's largest English language newspaper, and a book (in which I liberally praise Australia's governance system). I also have an online blog on *Times of India*.

Over these past six months I have written 17 articles about the pandemic. In the first of these on 6 March 2020 (entitled, "Age-based risk management of coronavirus"[66]) I wrote:

> despite innumerable unknowns about the virus, aggressive prevention of its spread is the best strategy. This doesn't mean we should lock down entire societies. Instead, we need a risk-based, data-driven approach that will minimise the spread of disease while facilitating economic activity.

On 24 March 2020 in an article entitled, "Lockdowns won't defeat the virus but will definitely destroy us all"[67] I wrote:

> Western governments are committing harakiri. Their cure is worse than the disease. Such mass-scale lockdowns will inevitably lead to an economic depression at which point no amount of bailouts or welfare measures will help.
>
> Instead, an age-based risk management policy can readily

---

[66] Sabhlok, Sanjeev, "Age-based risk management of coronavirus", *Times of India*, 6 March 2020. Short URL: https://bit.ly/3jqdWRm.

[67] Sabhlok, Sanjeev, "Lockdowns won't defeat the virus but will definitely destroy us all", *Times of India*, 24 March 2020. Short URL: https://bit.ly/2EHhujc.

flatten the curve even in the West, develop herd immunity and get rid of the virus within 12 months, regardless of whether science ultimately discovers a vaccine.

At that stage I was not aware of Sweden's approach but when I heard (on YouTube) Anders Tegnell say that lockdowns are against science, I was reassured that my analysis was correct.

To understand the science and its implications I studied the literature (both advanced textbooks and journal articles) on virology, immunology and epidemiology. I also looked through the WHO's plans and watched many videos where different experts explained their views. I was able to confirm that Tegnell's strategies were correct and that the Victorian Government had got it wrong.

The public servant is a citizen first

A public servant straddles two roles. He is a faceless soldier in the country's "civil army" but remains a citizen at all times. In that dual role he ensures – on behalf of the people – that the elected leaders follow the laws and the due process of policy making. When its role is performed well, the public service is the (largely unacknowledged) fifth pillar of society.

The core of public service is citizenship. The public servant's job, as the role clearly states, is to serve the public – in my case, the people of Victoria. He does "serve" the elected government of the day, but in doing so he provides it with independent advice. For example, just because something is an election commitment, a public servant doesn't need to support it. He must put down in writing any concerns he may have about it, and having done that – and as long as the election commitment is not too far off the scale of rationality and falls broadly within the ambit of the laws – he then advises the government on its implementation.

While people are familiar with the vigorous policy debates that take place in the media, even more robust debates occur all the time within the public service. These debates thrash out details and protect people's liberty unless it has become absolutely essential to restrict it for a justified reason.

There may come a time, however, when a public servant considers that the elected government is no longer serving the best interests of the people. At that point he can raise his concerns through the "proper channels", but once that fails, he must, as a citizen, voice his concerns directly to the people.

4.2 Capricious government: masks outdoors, the Police State and my resignation

As mentioned earlier, had the Victorian Government exercised the due diligence required by its own policy-making processes, published all information about the options available to it for dealing with the pandemic, and in doing so demonstrated that its heavy-handed lockdowns, curfews and mandatory mask requirements outdoors were essential, then I would have supported these measures. But they did not.

Instead, the Andrews Government has operated like a Star Chamber with no disclosure about the logic and reasons that underpin these lockdowns – which self-evidently violate Victoria's own pandemic plan.

The absurd outdoors mandatory mask policy

For the record, I am a mask maniac. Since late February 2020 I have been wearing a N95 mask, disposable gloves and a face shield in crowded settings. But I know that masks are unnecessary outdoors – particularly when no one else is around. I asked the Chief Health Officer via Twitter for his evidence for requiring masks outdoors. He has never responded.

But Victoria's law is clear on this. Exceptionally tight restrictions on the health officer's powers are built into on Victoria's *Public Health and Wellbeing Act 2008* (see the Box below).

Key provisions of the Public Health and Wellbeing Act 2008

Section 190 of the Victorian *Public Health and Wellbeing Act 2008* gives the Chief Health Officer significant powers but none of these are intended to be exercised arbitrarily. These powers are subject to powerful principles of justification and are time-limited.

Evidence needed

The Act states that public health measures must be based on evidence (Section 5: "decisions should be based on evidence available in the circumstances that is relevant and reliable").

People must be given full information

Section 8 requires that those who impose public health measures must provide full information and allow the public to participate: "Members of the public should be given access to reliable information in appropriate forms to facilitate a good understanding of public health issues" as well as "opportunities to participate in policy and program development".

Proportionality. Not arbitrary.

Section 9 of the Act prohibits arbitrary action: "decisions made and actions taken in the administration of this Act should be proportionate to the public health risk sought to be prevented, minimised or controlled; and should not be made or taken in an arbitrary manner".

Infectious disease prevention with minimum restrictions on rights.

Section 111 of the Act requires that "the spread of an infectious disease should be prevented or minimised with the minimum restriction on the rights of any person".

A 12-hour limit

190(6) of the Act states that "A direction under subsection (1)(b) to remain at any particular premises may be extended as many times as is reasonably necessary for the purpose of investigating, eliminating or reducing the risk to public health but so as not to exceed a continuous period of 12 hours".

By the way, I want to flag here my concern with the precautionary principle in Section 6 of the Act regarding which I will comment in the last chapter.

In my opinion, most pandemic directions issued by the Chief Health Officer to date violate Victoria's laws perhaps except those in which he may have thoroughly justified the intervention – but I'm not aware of any.

On 29 September 2020 it was reported that: "Asked why he would require Victorians to wear masks when there is no health purpose, Mr Andrews dismissed the question. 'That's an esoteric debate, isn't it? Maybe there will be a time when we have the luxury of having those debates.'"[68] Daniel Andrews has obviously not a shred of respect for Victoria's laws.

Expectedly, there has been a large inconsistency in enforcement. While walking in the park I am generally at a distance from other people that is vastly greater than Daniel Andrews (or his Chief Health Officer) is from journalists during his press conferences. But neither he nor his CHO wear a mask during these briefings.

Apparently, an exemption from wearing masks has been provided for media briefings because the hearing-impaired need to read lips. That's all very reasonable and I'm sure the CHO has peer-reviewed proof that proves in lab settings that this virus is particularly dangerous when I, Sanjeev Sabhlok, walk in the open air tens of metres from others but is intelligent enough to distinguish Daniel Andrews from others, and that when Mr Andrews opens his mouth the virus gets out of his way and goes back into its nano-sized shell. The full citation, please, Mr Sutton.

And the less said about the millions of dollars in fines that have been issued in Victoria, the better. Many fines are not being waived by the police

---

[68] Creighton, Adam, Tweet, 29 September, 2020. Short URL: https://bit.ly/2G7suHg.

on appeal despite legitimate reasons.[69] While citizens have the right to go to the Magistrates' Court to challenge a fine, I have not heard of many such challenges. Instead, some people on social media seem to think that hearings are being somehow obstructed. That seems unlikely to me but it is a matter for further investigation. I would imagine that no Magistrate would tolerate the mandates being issued by the CHO today which are not accompanied by appropriate justification.

My public condemnation of police brutalities

The mandatory mask decree in open spaces was the direct cause of events that led to widespread police brutalities in Victoria. These brutalities distressed me enormously. Even more distressing was that Daniel Andrews did not raise his voice against them. Instead, he blamed the people of Victoria. His Assistant Police Commissioner called the protestors against lockdowns a "tinfoil hat-wearing" brigade.

At that point, I ceased being largely neutral in my comments about the Victorian administration in my social media commentary (although I have long expressed stronger views regarding other nations) – and I started to escalate my commentary. I think I probably called Victoria a Police State. "Aggro" is the word that best comes to mind to describe what I have felt for some time now. There has been in my head a dark sense of foreboding and angst.

How could this happen?

And how can I watch this and keep quiet?

---

[69] Clayton, Rachel, "Victorian coronavirus fines not being reviewed properly, Melbourne community legal centres say", ABC News, 30 September 2020. Short URL: https://ab.co/2EIPVWz.

My resignation

The role of non-executive officers in the Victorian Public Service is to provide independent professional advice on policy matters. It is the executives who are then responsible for how that advice is processed and presented to the Treasurer.

My role in the Treasury was low profile. It suited me to work part-time in a non-executive role so that I could put most of my private-time effort into my governance reform mission for India. I was not a spokesperson for the Treasury, unlike Deputy Chief Health Officer Annaliese van Diemen who came under some controversy for a "woke" social media post (and was defended by Daniel Andrews) and who actually represented her department in the media.

My social media followers and friends have been mostly from India (and some from the USA). I do not even know who reads my social media posts in Australia. I don't know who would bother to link my criticism of lockdowns and the police state of Victoria with the Treasury position on this matter.

Nevertheless, on 9 September 2020, the Treasury asked me to remove any direct *and indirect* social media criticisms of the Victorian Government's pandemic policies. I was not provided with any specific post to delete. Until then, I had made very few direct criticisms of Victoria's policies but for many months I had vigorously challenged lockdown policies across the world. Were such attacks on lockdowns an "indirect" criticism of the Victorian Government's policy?

The VPS Code of Conduct[70] moderates the free speech rights of Victorian Public Service employees but these rights are not eliminated. Social media posts on topics that are unrelated to the policy area in which I provide professional advice do not violate the Code. I had also

---

[70] Victorian Public Service Commission, "Code of Conduct for Victorian Public Sector Employees", 1 June 2015. Short URL: https://bit.ly/2S3DEPr.

made it clear on my social media profiles that my views are personal and do not in any way represent the views of my employer.

I continue to believe a public servant in a non-executive role has the right to publicly question the actions of a government that violate the laws and sound principles, and especially when the foundations of civil society are being attacked – particularly in an area of policy unrelated to his or her professional role. Nevertheless, it became clear to me that a broken government cannot be fixed from within.

I love and admire everything about the Victorian Treasury but it became no longer possible to be a citizen and also to agree to be silenced. I had intended to work at the Treasury till age 65, if not 67. But that day I chose to resign within minutes of the meeting in which I was directed (that is the word used) to remove my posts.

My resignation process was completed on 10 September 2020.

4.3 Sliding towards authoritarian communism

The Great Hysteria has gone on for too long.

Although Daniel Andrews has finally withdrawn the curfew – which prohibited the people of Melbourne from leaving their homes between 9 pm (previously 8 pm) and 5 am – due to enormous public pressure, he has previously defended the curfew, arguing that it is "not about human rights. It is about human life".[71]

That was a specious argument. It is not one or the other. Life and liberty are of one piece.

Governments are required to protect life and liberty and everything

---

[71] McGowan, Michael, "Daniel Andrews dismisses human rights complaint over Melbourne Covid curfew", *The Guardian*, 11 September 2020. Short URL: https://bit.ly/2G1MEIM.

else we entrust them with. We do not contribute 40% of our income (Commonwealth, State and local) to fund our government only to look after a tiny sliver of our interests.

I am aware that history offers us no assurance of the sustained progress of liberty, even in the West. Aware of the challenges to its spread, John Stuart Mill noted that advances in freedom occur slowly. Hayek observed that "[t]here has never been a time when liberal ideals were fully realized, and when liberalism did not look forward to further improvement of institutions". But probably neither of them imagined the course of human liberty could be reversed so sharply and so quickly.

We are seeing Victoria slide towards full-blown communism. This is not an exaggeration. At least three characteristics typical of societies like the USSR are now found in Victoria.

First, centralised planning. The lockdown orders issued by the Andrews government over the past months look very similar to orders that a central planner would make. Some businesses are allowed to remain open because some busybody bureaucrat somewhere thinks they are "essential". Others, not so fortunate, have seen their operations shut down either entirely or partially, or are told to comply with absurd rules that have no justification. Detailed reasons are never provided. Jim's Mowing is a case in point. Alan Jones has ridiculed many other such rules in his TV program.

Second, fear psychosis. The fear psychosis created in the community by police brutalities in Victoria is unprecedented. Never has such mass-scale internment of an entire population occurred in human history.

Michel Foucault's exploration of infectious disease as a way to create an all-encompassing government might hold some clues. It seems almost as if governments across the world salivated when the pandemic came. Such are their dreams: "Each individual is fixed in his place. And, if he moves, he does so at the risk of his life, contagion or punishment".[72]

Good medicine is about providing comfort and reassurance to patients and being driven by reason. But the media and politicians have made people believe that the virus has taken hundreds of times more lives than it actually has.[73] Patients have been so terrorised they are reluctant to get their health checked.

A registered nurse who had grown up in a "totalitarian country of Eastern Europe" wrote to me recently about the chaos prevailing in Victoria's health system, where "everyone is [now] obsessed by and preoccupied [with] finding ways [to] pass on accountability and responsibility to someone else". That's precisely what happens when people are fearful of the government. Instead of focusing on health care, our health professionals are now focused on trying to escape blame.

Third, preference falsification. This is when people hide their true opinions in order to remain socially acceptable or to mislead the authorities. Timur Kuran, my professor at the University of Southern California during my doctoral studies, had written a book in 1995 entitled, *Private Truth, Public Lies*. He shows how preference falsification is a chronic feature of communist societies. Today, hundreds of people are writing to me in private commending my stand but they will not speak out in public lest their career is impacted or family and friends ostracise them. This is preference falsification.

There are other examples, such as Daniel Andrews's supportive approach towards the communist Black Lives Matter protestors in June 2020, yet a harsh approach against anti-lockdown protesters in August 2020.

---

[72] Sarasin, Philipp, "Understanding the Coronavirus Pandemic with Foucault?", Foucaultblog, 31 March 2020. Short URL: https://bit.ly/367tg1G.
[73] KEKST CNC, "COVID-19 Opinion Tracker", 10th-15th July 2020, Edition 4. Short URL: https://bit.ly/307pFN4.

If we are not living in a full-blown communist state yet, we are hurtling towards it.

4.4 Loss of society's moral compass

It goes without saying that coercive lockdowns are viscerally immoral. We can look at this issue in a number of ways.

Science does not adjudicate on moral principles

Science cannot throw light on a moral course of action for society. In response to one of my tweets, Professor Graham Medley said on 26 September 2020: "Both the disease and the interventions are damaging. Science can't solve this problem. [S]cience [can] help to solve technical issues but it can't balance freedom vs economics vs health"[74].

Fortunately, since there was no scientific paper published before 2020 recommending lockdowns, there was never any real contest in this case between the originally approved public health plans and liberty.

Golden rule

We can test the lockdowns against the Golden rule: Do unto others as you would have them do unto you. This tells us that we each have the right to lock ourselves up at home for as long as we wish but we are not free to lock others. We can wear as many masks and protective equipment that we want to wear outdoors but we are not free to compel others to do so. And if we are scared of someone approaching us in a public park, we can move away. The Golden rule does not justify lockdowns.

---

[74] Medley, Graham, Tweet, 26 September 2020. Short URL: https://bit.ly/2S3mLoh.

Citizenship

Lockdowns are an affront to the concept of citizenship. The philosopher Riccardo Manzottia has observed about these lockdowns that "[t]he government should not take ownership of the lives of the citizens, for then they are no longer citizens"[75]. We are now pawns on Daniel Andrews's chessboard. Or maybe we are his personally owned battery hens – or possibly his ant farm.

There can be no citizenship without freedom

These constraints are all the more galling when we see the Swedes being trusted by their government to act responsibly. In some (superficial) ways the actions taken by the people of Sweden and Australia are similar – except that the Swedes were told the reasons and advised to social distance and protect the elderly. So they did not experience any fear psychosis, mental trauma or lack of agency. They remained free to wear a mask outdoors if they wished, but no one stomped on their head with a boot if they chose not to. The helplessness to which Australians have been subjected makes a mockery of the idea that we are citizens.

Decency

Finally, there is the issue of decency. While Manzottia's exploration of citizenship addresses this matter to some extent, there is the broader question of how we can build and sustain a free and flourishing, decent society.

When I visit my GP, he offers me a huge welcoming grin that relaxes and calms me down. Likewise, our interactions with other humans are

---

[75] Swarna Bharat Party, "Economist Nils Karlson and philosopher Riccardo Manzotti strongly defend the Swedish approach", YouTube, 8 January 2020. Short URL: https://bit.ly/33XlC7d.

underpinned by a strong expectation of decency.

But in Victoria the foundational trust between people and the government has been degraded, if not shattered. The same applies to our trust in others. The loss of decency prompted by these lockdowns perhaps led some of our police to feel emboldened to snatch an elderly lady's mobile phone.

4.5 Loss of agency and the right to work

The last thing in my mind when I came to Australia in December 2000 was that this nation would so dramatically, rapidly and on such a mammoth scale, subvert the most fundamental liberties – of occupation, of movement, and even breathing fresh air outdoors.

The destruction of the right to occupation has been one of the most troublesome. This right is about our right to agency and to earn a living from our effort and creation. Our existence, identity and self-respect are intimately tied up with our livelihood. This right has now been radically restricted in Australia for a vast number of businesses. These entrepreneurs, property owners, and workers have been shunted, instead, to the dole – something no self-respecting person wants to have any part of.

The other day someone I was talking to was surprised that someone with "libertarian" views is (or now, was) employed by the Treasury. But all economists are "libertarian" to a certain degree. The discipline of economics is about the defence of individual agency and minimising the role of government. The default position of all good economists is to let people do what they think is best in their own self-interest, for that is the best way to help everyone achieve happiness and prosperity.

Only when we harm others in the course of our free actions (through what is called "market failure") does any economist seek to get involved and consider government intervention. When a market failure is demonstrated, economists then spend much of their time identifying the least intrusive or "light-handed" way to address the failure. We believe that the "invisible hand" of markets works best in most cases. Any "hand of the government" – which on its own is unable to produce anything of value – must be very light, a velvet glove; just enough to minimise harms.

Economists are also keenly aware of the concept of "government failure" – the failure arising from government over-reach and flawed thinking. In general, "line" experts such as in health, town planning, education or environment, do not necessarily understand markets and liberty. Often with the best of intentions, they propose schemes to impose enormous burdens and harms on society instead of facilitating the markets. The reason the Treasury has more than a hundred economists is to apply a blowtorch to such grandiose plans.

Risk-based and performance-based frameworks are a critical part of this defence of liberty. Had such frameworks (which are part of the DNA of Victorian policy making) been applied during this pandemic none of the mass-scale closures of workplaces would have happened. When good policy is rejected, liberty is also lost.

4.6 The institutions of Australia seem to be fraying at the edge

It is not just the governments that have lost their way. Key Australia institutions seem to be fraying at the edge.

Political parties

Unlike Australia, the USA still seems has strong voices for liberty at its helm. The US Attorney General William Barr recently said that "other than slavery, which was a different kind of restraint," coronavirus lockdowns were the "greatest intrusion on civil liberties in American history".

Australia's politicians have never said that. And although Victoria's opposition party, the Liberal Party, showed some spine in resisting the extension of Victoria's emergency powers, its leaders have not yet called out the Andrews Government's policies. They have not demanded the disclosure of the government's policy objectives and why Andrews is not implementing his own pandemic plan.

Media

The media in Australia remains a mixed bag. Most of the mainstream media appear to have become the broadcasting arm of the government. It does not ask questions nor does it analyse issues in depth. It needs to lift its game.

Business

Finally, what is the business community waiting for? Do they want things to go entirely bust before they start organising resistance? While there may be reputational consequences for a business leader who steps out to challenge the established narrative, it is time at least for business associations to speak out.

5
Why did the Victorian Government lose its head?

Why did the Victorian Government lose its head? Pandemics naturally cause hysteria but as far as I know mass hysteria of this kind, and mass imprisonment of society, has never been seen before.

5.1 Why did Victoria abandon its pandemic plan?

It will be a matter for a future Royal Commission to identify precisely when and how the Victorian pandemic plan was abandoned. But I venture to offer preliminary leads.

It is possible that the sequence of events evolved along the following lines:

1) Neil Ferguson's 16 March 2020 projection of the path of the

pandemic.

2) The media loved the scare and drummed up panic.

3) Direct indoctrination by Chinese "experts" brought into Italy.

4) The WHO's praise for China's lockdowns.

5) The UK politicians buckled first and jumped into the well.

6) Our politicians then followed their "mother country" faithfully down the hole.

1) Role of Neil Ferguson's modelling

It is possible that Neil Ferguson's 16 March 2020 Imperial College paper, entitled, "Impact of non-pharmaceutical interventions (NPIs) to reduce Covid-19 mortality and healthcare demand"[76] might have had something to do with the progression of events. (Neil Ferguson was the lead author with 30 other co-authors. But as he has been the main spokesperson so, for the sake of simplicity, I will cite him as the paper's author in book.)

Although the paper was not peer-reviewed and although its model's source code was not published, his findings were treated as highly significant by the global media. For instance, the *Washington Post* reported on 18 March 2020[77]:

> The new forecasts, by Neil Ferguson and his colleagues at the Imperial College COVID-19 Response Team, were quickly

---

[76] Ferguson, Neil M, et. al. "Impact of non-pharmaceutical interventions (NPIs) to reduce Covid-19 mortality and healthcare demand", 16 March 2020. Short URL: https://bit.ly/3cvm4O3.

[77] Booth, William, "A chilling scientific paper helped upend U.S. and U.K. coronavirus strategies", *Washington Post*, 18 March 2020. Short URL: https://wapo.st/2Sp4EZY

endorsed by Johnson's government to design new and more extreme measures to suppress the spread of the virus.

The Imperial College London group reported that if nothing was done by governments and individuals and the pandemic remained uncontrolled, 510,000 would die in Britain and 2.2 million in the United States over the course of the outbreak.

It is hard to imagine a more innocuous cause of a Great Hysteria than an academic paper. It also appears that while there were a number of other, less "scary" estimates in the paper, the media chose the scariest projections which then stuck for many months in the minds of the people.

Although I was not aware of it at that stage, it is well-known among those who study such things that virtually all epidemiological models have a long history of over-estimating risks. The media obviously did not have anyone with the training of Richard Epstein[78] to ask questions, so the worst-case scenario appears to have become the most likely scenario in the minds of the people.

Johan Giesecke, the former chief scientist for the European Centre for Disease Control and Prevention, was quick to oppose Ferguson's calamitous estimates. On 28 March 2020 he said that Ferguson's model is "one of the most wrong" papers ever published.[79] Later, Anders Tegnell of Sweden got the model investigated by his team and has repeatedly stated in the media that he does not agree with Ferguson's findings.

---

[78] Epstein, Richard A., "Monday, March 23, 2020reduce COVID-19 mortality and healthcare demand", Hoover Institution, 23 March 2020. Short URL: https://hvr.co/3j56mvo.

[79] Rushton, Katherine, and Foggo, Daniel, "Neil Ferguson, the scientist who convinced Boris Johnson of UK coronavirus lockdown, criticised in past for flawed research", *The Telegraph*, 28 March 2020. Short URL: https://bit.ly/33mkpXV

To get a sense of how wrong Ferguson' upper end estimate was, here's what a 29 July 2020 article reported[80]:

> On May 10, Dagens Nyheter – Sweden's biggest daily newspaper – analysed a pair of models inspired by the Imperial College of London study, which predicted as many as 40 million people could die if the coronavirus was left unchecked. The models predicted that Sweden's ICUs (intensive care units) would expire before May and nearly 100,000 people would die from COVID-19 by July.
>
> "Our model predicts that, using median infection-fatality-rate estimates, at least 96,000 deaths would occur by 1 July without mitigation," the authors wrote.
>
> Total COVID-19 deaths in Sweden stand at 5,700, nearly 90,000 less than modellers predicted. Hospitals were never overrun. Daily deaths in Sweden have slowed to a crawl. The health agency reports no new ICU admissions.

As at the time of writing this book, total COVID-19 deaths in Sweden now stand at 5,893. Sweden did not impose lockdowns without which Ferguson apparently thought they would face calamity. Instead, Sweden followed well-established science to flatten the curve through voluntary social distancing and age-based risk management.

Reports suggest that Sweden's overall death rate this year per million is tracking close to its average death rate for the past five years. The overall death rate in Sweden this year is also not very different to death rates in previous "bad flu" years. So much for Ferguson's upper-end estimates.

Recently, the scientist Mike Yeadon has said that "no serious scientist

---

[80] Miltimore, Jon, "Sweden's Actual COVID-19 Results Compared to What Modelers Predicted in April", Foundation for Economic Freedom, 28 July 2020. Short URL: https://bit.ly/3inEJMK.

gives any validity" to Ferguson's model.[81] "It's important that you know most scientists don't accept that it [Ferguson's model] was even faintly right...but the government is still wedded to the model".

But these debates among professional scientists would not have mattered had Ferguson's model not been picked up by the media. It is not possible to place the blame for the Great Hysteria on Neil Ferguson. He surely did not intend it. Like any other academic, he put out a paper. The media has much explaining to do.

It also appears that similar over-estimates were being churned within Victoria by a few well-known institutes. Any future Royal Commission must investigate whether the models used by the Victorian Government were scientifically valid. More importantly, whether Treasury officials (many of whom have significant mathematical skills) were involved in cross-checking these models, or did groupthink prevail.

2) The role of the media

In previous pandemics the media was aware of its own impact on society and acted with a sense of responsibility in reporting deaths. It was noted in *The Lancet* on 25 May 2020 that[82]:

> At the end of July, 1957, the Daily Mail issued a dire warning about a "new outbreak of Asian flu" when a 1-year-old girl fell ill in Fulham. The Guardian surrendered its cool editorial tone for a headline reading: "Crash Fight Against Asian 'Flu'".

---

[81] Lopez, Ralph, "Former Chief Science Officer for Pfizer Says 'Second Wave' Faked on False-Positive COVID Tests, "Pandemic is Over'", HubPages, 1 October 2020. Short URL: https://bit.ly/2RZZV0F.

[82] Honigsbaum, Mark, "Revisiting the 1957 and 1968 influenza pandemics", *The Lancet*, 25 May 2020. Short URL: https://bit.ly/33kvpoX.

However, such headlines were the exception and for the most part newspapers seem to have behaved responsibly during the pandemic. Publishers were also reluctant to be seen to be stoking public fears.

But this time around, the media has behaved differently. Without the daily drumming up of the panic by the media, it is doubtful that we would have had the Great Hysteria.

Why has the media seemingly lost its sense of proportion and much of its ethics?

I venture to suggest that this state of affairs is at least partly attributable to the fact that mainstream media is in its death throes. Its revenues have plummeted due to stiff competition from social media and private blogs. Worse, the "sane" journalists can't attract enough "clicks" and are therefore being guided out of the door. The ones left behind are those who are inclined to be hysterical but they are successful in driving "eyeballs" and revenues.

Fear is an extremely powerful emotion, deeply etched into the human limbic system. We are perfectly programmed to be hyper-reactive receptacles for panicky "news". We hear, "Wolf, Wolf!" and without hesitating, run first to gather our sheep.

Neil Ferguson (and his co-authors) inadvertently put the matchlight to our fear and the media doused it with petrol. It was now a blazing inferno. And a huge feast for the media. The moolah rolled in like the heavens had parted. For a few weeks I myself became a pair of "eyeballs", watching YouTube news channels every evening from around the world. A flood of advertisement revenues must have poured into media coffers.

Marc Siegel's 2005 book, *False Alarm*, looked at some recent fears: the anthrax scare and fears about smallpox and gas bioterrorism agents that arose after the 11 September 2001 attacks in the USA, as well as the

SARS epidemic and the mad cow disease. In each case we managed as a species to blow the threats out of all proportion.

The only way out of this fearful mess is through our higher brain, by seeking information that gives us a better handle on the risk. But science is not of much use here. Most scientists know nothing about the human mind and are happy to add fuel to the fire. Siegel shows how the CDC "attached itself to the media megaphone and made us afraid to open our mail" during the anthrax scare. Likewise, in this current pandemic, the WHO fueled the hysteria and ignored its own published recommendations.

The net result of all this is that the people of the world have been scared witless. An opinion poll company, Kekst CNC found in July 2020[83] that the average person in the UK, USA, France, Sweden and Germany thinks that 100 to 300 times more people have died from this virus than it has actually killed.

But Charles Mackay wrote: "Men, it has been well said, think in herds; it will be seen that they go mad in herds, while they only recover their senses slowly, and one by one". That is how all hysterias end – one person at a time.

So, this hysteria, too, will one day come to an end. Its amazing path of devastation with the non-COVID-19 deaths (even as it was a godsend for media moguls) will no doubt be analysed by scholars from a range of disciplines for many decades to come.

Does this mean that I oppose what the media did this time? No. I think that's how the competitive private sector works. It is never perfect.

But that's why we pay 40% of our earnings to the government in taxes – to hire hyper-rational people like me to provide rock-solid advice regardless

---

[83] KEKST CNC, "COVID-19 Opinion Tracker", 10th-15th July 2020, Edition 4. Short URL: https://bit.ly/307pFN4.

of any media circus that might be playing out there. The problem is not that the media drummed up the hysteria but that governments dumped their own plans.

3) China's suspect role

The third reason was perhaps the Chinese government itself. China had been stung by world-wide criticism on many fronts including by the WHO.

But keen to show the world that it had done the "right" thing, China pulled all diplomatic levers. It applied pressure on Italy. On 11 March 2020[84] the Italian Foreign Minister Di Maio told China's Foreign Minister Wang Yi that Italy was "paying close attention to and learning from" China's experience with the virus.

Did China influence Australia, as well? We know that Daniel Andrews has been a bit too close to China. The possibility of China's undue influence in Victoria will be a matter for a future Royal Commission.

4) The ideological Director-General of WHO

The fourth factor is the WHO chief Tedros Adhanom Ghebreyesus.

The science that WHO has published on its website is clear: it is against lockdowns. WHO's China representative, Gauden Galea, also made clear on 24 January 2020 that lockdowns are "certainly not a recommendation the WHO has made".

And it appears that Ghebreyesus initially distanced himself from the lockdowns.

---

[84] Khaliq, Riyaz ul, "Chinese doctors to help Italy against coronavirus", Anadolu Agency, 11 March 2020. Short URL: https://bit.ly/3i4DWjQ.

But then Ghebreyesus started praising China's policies.

Now, science, particularly public health science, should never be done on the run. Ghebreyesus should never have flipped on the WHO's unequivocal recommendations against lockdowns. Either he had suddenly gained scientific information of unbelievable value that led him to change WHO's recommendation. Or he was driven by ideology.

Since he did not publish any paper proving that lockdowns work, we can conclude that he was influenced by ideology. It appears that Ghebreyesus has a communist background in Ethiopia.

Now that he has set the West ablaze, Ghebreyesus is sitting on the sidelines, watching the West burn. If he is not the enemy of the West, he needs to speak out in support of the ideas I have presented in this book and help to douse the panic – at once.

It is certain that had any other scientist, such as Anders Tegnell, been the head of the WHO, we would never have seen these lockdowns. It is also clear that groupthink is rampant within the WHO since no one from within that organisation has come out to refute Ghebreyesus's radical shift in recommendations.

5,6) The role of UK and Australian politicians

Unlike in Sweden where the highly experienced and bookish-looking Tegnell was given charge of the country's pandemic policy, in other countries the politicians wanted to become heroes to save us all. Every life was suddenly equally important, they told us.

To be charitable to them, it is possible that after the mass hysteria had built up in late March, the politicians were no longer in a position to push back. Had they allowed technical people to implement the pre-defined pandemic plan (like in Sweden), they might have been able to evade the challenge of directly explaining the policy to the people. But since they had chosen to become the "face" of the policy, they were faced with a Hobson's choice. The hysteria was too excessive. If they tried to un-scare the people their popularity could plummet.

They needed an out. Two factors probably came into consideration:

- *The precautionary principle*: Not many Australians are aware of it, but there is this extraordinarily dangerous principle embedded in much of Australian legislation, which empowers governments to abandon all reason and do whatever they wish. This extremely infamous "precautionary principle" (which I'll discuss in the last chapter) also happens to be embedded within public health legislation. It is possible that Daniel Andrews was advised that he could resort to this principle as well as to Victoria's emergency powers to legally abandon Victoria's pandemic plan.

- *The difficulty of identifying harm and apportioning blame*: Peter Singer has identified another important matter. Politicians were aware that the harms from lockdowns are likely to be delayed and difficult to identify except through statistical analysis. People wouldn't just die off immediately because of lockdowns. The longer-term deaths would not be salient. Scholars might add up the harms of lockdowns and report them in some obscure academic journal two years down the line but that would not be front page news. And it would be hard to attribute these harms to any specific politician.

Regardless of the reasoning the politicians used, the UK fell first. Once it fell, its tributary states – Australia, Canada and New Zealand – fell like dominos.

Then things became truly perverse. In the UK, behavioural "scientists" made a particularly devilish recommendation on 22 March 2020[85] – to actively stir up hysteria and scare the people (this was the sum and essence of what it said in bureaucratic jargon). This was probably picked up in Victoria and might explain why we got such alarmist government advertisements. Not once did the Victorian Government's messaging reflect the age-based risk profile of the pandemic or even provide any balanced presentation of the facts.

So, everything that could have stopped the Great Hysteria fell by the wayside. There was no hope after that.

The questions arise: Are our politicians evil? Was there a conspiracy?

I believe that the much simpler explanation outlined above might work better. Governments are hierarchical and dramatically prone to groupthink. They are also prone to unbelievable stupidity (the public choice literature has explored this at length). And on top of all that, the road to Hell is paved with good intentions.

5.2 The Swedes followed their plan and did not buckle to the hysteria

It has been amazing to look at Sweden over the past six months while the world has been burning. Sweden has remained a calm, staid and peaceful society, managing its life almost as if nothing much has happened. It has been almost like a different planet.

Sweden has suffered a lot as well. Pandemics are not easy. But by now life is getting back to normal.

Anders Tegnell has been going around for the past six months, explaining patiently to anyone who cares to listen, that science is against lock-

---

[85] Robinson, Mike, "COVID Coercion: Boris Johnson's Psychological Attack on the UK Public", UK Column, 14 May 2020. Short URL: https://bit.ly/348ns5s.

downs. There is a little bit more, though. At least some of Sweden's approach to human dignity and liberty is an outcome of its Constitution, which I will touch upon in the last chapter.

Basically, it appears that the management of pandemic is like a 12-round boxing match that only ends when the virus is knocked out – either through natural herd immunity or a vaccine. Dodging the virus through lockdowns imposes a huge cost, including health costs, but doesn't knock off the virus.

Johan Giesecke said an important thing when people were haranguing him about Sweden's death toll in April: "Ask me this question after one year", he said, "when all nations would have roughly the same death rates". The only difference in a year's time, one could deduce from his message, is that the Swedish economy would have long recovered – without costing a single additional death from lockdowns and also enabling it to save far more lives in the future – while other nations would have become much poorer, hence unable to save lives from a myriad of other causes.

It is a testament to the brilliance of Anders Tegnell that Sweden's death rate per million is now 14th from the top – with nations with higher death rates than Sweden having imposed severe lockdowns. Lockdowns did not help anyone in any way.

In this context, we must note that Sweden has a particularly high elderly population – over 20% of its population is over 65. And its nursing homes are very tightly and densely populated. Between a third to a half of Sweden's deaths initially occurred in these nursing homes. Later, by tightly clamping down on the nursing homes, Sweden managed to reduce further COVID-19 deaths. This is therefore clear, that an age-based risk management strategy *can* work very well, but only if a government puts a lot of resources into it.

Sweden has refused to undertake mass-testing. The standard science is clear: that testing should only be done once someone is admitted to hospital. The government's focus should be to minimise harm, not to keep testing. Testing merely fuels hysteria. And the shoddy nature of PCR tests has meant that the media has kept giving oxygen to an unhinged obsession with "cases".

We are now hearing reports that Victoria will soon introduce mass testing. This is wrong on so many levels it is hard to begin. It is unscientific and unhinged because tests create hysteria, they are unnecessary, they are costly, and they invade privacy.

As the Swedish immunologist Henrik Branden has pointed out, "The virus has spread all over the world. It is completely impossible to lock this virus again". It is here to stay. We need a way to live with it and minimise harm without causing ourselves additional harm. Since a thoroughly tested vaccine remains a pipe dream, a moon shot, it is far better to target natural herd immunity.

6
Call for action: Immediate actions

First, the government must stop scaring people. Second, it must un-scare people. It must also do all these things, below – right now.

6.1 Lift the lockdowns, open the borders and work with industry to create risk-based solutions

The mandatory lockdowns must go *entirely*. Everything must be allowed to re-start – voluntarily. And *all* borders must open, not just in Victoria but across Australia (including the international border).

Those who wish to resume work, should be allowed to do so. Shops that wish to re-open, should be allowed to open. There should, of course, be no compulsion to work or to re-open.

> We need to start developing herd immunity in a staggered manner.

- The government should switch 80 per cent of its focus to protecting the elderly. We must cocoon the elderly and vulnerable and let the virus spread in a controlled manner.

- Restrictions on the professional judgement of the medical profession must be immediately removed. There are reasons to believe that drugs like Hydroxychloroquine (HCQ) have been helpful in countries like India in saving lives. A doctor has written to me that "evidence shows ventilator use was not most beneficial". Why don't we let doctors at the coal face decide?

- There should be voluntary recommendations for social distancing (including wearing masks in crowded places), that take into account the risk profile of people. Let those who are old or have co-morbidities take additional precautions.

- The government should put out information on ways for people to supplement their immune system, such as through Vitamin D.

- Industry should be supported through co-regulation to work out its own solutions to the risks.

This will bring us largely in line with Sweden's approach (i.e. our own original approach).

6.2 A vaccine may no longer be needed, like with all previous pandemics

On 2 April 2020, Scott Morrison spoke about a coronavirus vaccine becoming available in six months.[86] That was the timeframe set out for lockdowns. But that was in direct contradiction both to the WHO and to his own Deputy Chief Health officer who said that a vaccine would

---

[86] Brown, Greg, "Scott Morrison wary on setting 'reopening' target", *The Australian*, 2 April 2020. Short URL: https://bit.ly/3kTjiFh.

take 18 months "to develop"[87] – let alone produce the 16 billion doses the world needs (assuming a multi-dosed vaccine).

Six months later, politicians are desperate for a vaccine to salvage their careers. There is speculation that "something" will become available soon, but we have no assurance.

I believe politicians have fallen for the sunk cost fallacy. They have already caused so much havoc by waiting for a vaccine, they think they should cause just a little bit more damage and the vaccine will miraculously appear.

The prospect of a vaccine remains exceptionally slim, a moon shot. Four coronaviruses give us the common cold but we have never had a vaccine for any of them. There have recently been two more: SARS (SARS-CoV-1) in 2002–2004 and the Middle East respiratory syndrome coronavirus (MERS-CoV) in 2012. The vaccines developed for SARS provided some protective immunity but they also resulted in an immune disease in animals. As a result, "no human studies were done, nor were the vaccine studies taken further because the virus disappeared".[88] As far as MERS is concerned, there is no vaccine for it to date, eight years down the track.[89]

Ian Frazer, an Australian immunologist has said: "In my lifetime, I can count seven new viruses that have arrived and we don't have vaccines for

---

[87] McCauley, Dana, "'Experimental' coronavirus vaccine months away, pinprick tests in doubt", *The Age*, 1 April 2020. Short URL: https://bit.ly/33YeS96.

[88] Roossinck, Marilyn J., "The mysterious disappearance of the first SARS virus, and why we need a vaccine for the current one but didn't for the other", *The Conversation*, 5 May 2020. Short URL: https://bit.ly/3kRahwq.

[89] Wikipedia, "Middle East respiratory syndrome". Short URL: https://bit.ly/2SnEiYd.

most of them yet".[90]

What if a vaccine is never found? Johan Giesecke asked New Zealand and Australia policymakers in April 2020: "what do you do for the next 30 years? Will you close your borders completely? Quarantine everyone who is going to Australia or New Zealand? Because the disease will be out there".[91]

The biggest problem with waiting for a vaccine, of course, is that it was never part of any approved plan. This apparent wait for a vaccine while everyone is forced indoors at the point of a gun has become part of a mass-scale human experiment (lockdowns) that violates the Nuremberg Code.

Here is the good news. Most countries (not Australia) *no longer need a vaccine*. Most pandemics are self-limiting as I have explained earlier, due to herd immunity which degrades them into seasonal infections. In this case, as we have seen, herd immunity has largely been achieved in many parts of the world (not Australia) and a second or third wave is increasingly unlikely.

Australia should not wait for a vaccine but move towards staggered and risk-based herd immunity.

6.3 Vaccine must not be mandatory when it does arrive

There are at least two problems with a fast-tracked COVID-19 vaccine. First, there have been a number of reports that some vaccine projects are skipping animal trials in the interest of speed. But the SARS coronavirus

---

[90] Passi, Sacha, "Renowned immunologist Professor Ian Frazer says coronavirus must 'run its course'", 9Now, undated ("six months ago" as at 2 October 2020). Short URL: https://bit.ly/2GagaFW.

[91] Sky News, "Former Chief Scientist reveals coronavirus 'is going on all around us'", YouTube, 29 April 2020. Short URL: https://bit.ly/2GBlJ0o.

vaccine failed animal trials. So, why is skipping animal trials considered to be a good idea? Second, based on the experience with flu, a vaccine might actually not be of much help to the most vulnerable segment of the population: the elderly.

It is crucial therefore to focus more on therapeutic drugs and treatments (and to ensure Vitamin D sufficiency among the people). The main issue, though, is that everyone must have the right to choose whether they wish to take the vaccine when it is finally approved. Except in the case of an extremely lethal virus like smallpox which can actually be eradicated with concerted effort (and has been eradicated), all other vaccines must always be voluntary.

I am a huge fan of vaccines. Jenner and Salk are my heroes. I regularly take the flu shot, even though I know it is not effective across the entire population. But in this case, as far as I am concerned, I will prefer the politicians and doctors take the vaccine first – along with their entire family: then watch for three months and decide.

6.4 No mass testing

There are some extremist epidemiologists who keep advocating "mass testing" as an alternative to lockdowns. But the only thing they have to go on is their mathematical models which are the purest form of garbage invented by man.

I have studied this matter including engaging extensively with an epidemiologist and his models, and written against mass testing.[92] The proper course is to test (like we do for any other disease) only when a person suffers extreme consequences and is hospitalised.

---

[92] Sabhlok, Sanjeev, "Testing and contact tracing can't eradicate SARS-CoV-2 – Part 2", *Times of India*, 3 May 2020. Short URL: https://bit.ly/36lxd2X. Part 1 is available at: https://bit.ly/34l1g7Z.

Mass testing is not recommended by the WHO's 2019 guidelines. Doing so is therefore yet another mass human experiment that violates the Nuremberg Code and all codes of ethics in science. It is a criminal act and must not be allowed to be imposed.

6.5 How concerned should we be about the long-term effects of COVID-19?

People keep asking me about the "long haulers" – those who are continuing to suffer a range of symptoms long after they first caught COVID-19. How concerned should we be?

It is a fact that recovering from this virus takes longer, on average, than from other similar viruses. But I am not persuaded about claims that "Overall, approximately 10% of people who've had COVID-19 experience prolonged symptoms"[93]. This smacks of exaggeration.

We do know one thing – that millions of people including major sports stars have fully recovered from this novel coronavirus and are doing perfectly fine. The news reports suggest that some of the recovered major sports stars are back to their sport with full vigour.

Further we know that this is not the only virus to leave behind long term effects in a few cases. Mike Yeadon[94] notes that "although COVID can have serious after-effects, so can flu or any respiratory illness". SARS, another coronavirus, also had some cases with long term effects.

There is a problem, as well, with the current data about this condition.

---

[93] Rubin, Rita, "As Their Numbers Grow, COVID-19 "Long Haulers" Stump Experts", JAMA Network, 23 September 2020. Short URL: https://bit.ly/3cFyDq0.

[94] Lopez, Ralph, "Former Chief Science Officer for Pfizer Says 'Second Wave' Faked on False-Positive COVID Tests, 'Pandemic is Over'", HubPages, 1 October 2020. Short URL: https://bit.ly/2RZZV0F.

It appears that "[m]any long haulers never had laboratory confirmation of COVID-19". We need robust data and robust studies before we start considering this issue to be a major concern.

Novel coronavirus is not a mild virus. It can be quite nasty. We must take reasonable precautions. But we should not use the possibility of some cases which will have long term effects (an Act of Nature) as an excuse to harm those who do not or will not have any such effects (through lockdowns, an Act of Man). Collateral damage of other humans is *always* a crime.

7
Call for action: Longer term actions

> *Power tends to corrupt, and absolute power corrupts absolutely.*
> John Dalberg-Acton

For months we haven't had a government "for the people". Our trust in parliamentarians has gone.

I am more against big government now than I was at any point in my life. We must act to bring about small government in our lifetime: a night watchman state. In this last chapter I will outline the more important fundamental reforms of the laws and governance system we need in order to embed the lessons learnt from the Great Hysteria into our institutional DNA.

Many of these reforms do not need to wait for a Royal Commission's report. Any major political party that includes these reforms in its manifesto will get my support – I might even join that party to personally

105

explain these reforms to the people and help deliver them through the various Parliaments of Australia.

7.1 Revoke peacetime emergency powers of all governments

The plenary power of State governments means that they can do whatever they want. The few checks and balances through the State Parliament and democratic processes that we have, have functioned like a house of straw to protect a pig from the Big Bad Wolf. Common law and the courts have also failed to protect us.

We need constitutional change.

Underpinning the civilised approach Sweden took is its Constitution which does not allow the imposition of emergency powers (and hence the suspension of liberties) except in the case of war. As noted by Behrang Kianzad and Timo Minssen in a 12 May 2020 article, "the Constitution protects Swedish citizens from blanket limitations of freedom of movement or general stay home orders".

Summarising its approach, Mark Klamberg, a professor in international law at Stockholm University wrote on 9 April 2020 that "Sweden has chosen a rule-of-law approach as opposed to an approach where the Sovereign (i.e. the government) is totally unrestrained in time of crisis".

Any restrictions on individual liberty in Sweden must be proportionate and based on laws enacted in advance of a public health crisis. Its laws specify that the courts must agree to any restraint on each specific individual on public health grounds. The CMO has to petition the courts for mandatory testing of a suspected ill individual and if someone is proven ill then the CMO must petition the courts for the isolation of the infected individuals.

It is true that Sweden amended its laws in recent months to allow the imposition of certain wider restrictions, such as on an entire business precinct, but most of these powers have not been exercised, possibly because these laws might have been challenged and found by Sweden's courts to violate its Constitution.

Sweden's approach confirms that there is no basis in a free society for trade-offs between public health and liberty. In free societies, the rights of the real sovereigns (us citizens) must remain paramount at all times.

On 9 April 2020, concerned deeply with the way the world was going, Wendy Parmet (who has been raising an alarm against public health oppressions for some time) asked for an overhaul of public health laws: "With Covid-19 in our communities, the time has come to imagine and implement public health laws that emphasize support rather than restriction".

In a very important 260-page report issued on 18 August 2020 entitled, Assessing Legal Responses to COVID-19[95], 50 law experts (Parmet is on the editorial committee) have made recommendations to better respond to pandemics. Among the suggested actions is that "State legislatures should amend or enact new public health legislation clarifying the scope and authority of state officials to limit person-to-person interaction and impose closures, movement restrictions, gathering bans, and physical distancing requirements".

Further, the report recommends that "every emergency declaration should include the following information: specific epidemiological data supporting the order; specific requirements for social distancing and mask wearing; an explanation of why the order is needed; and an explanation of why the order does not violate personal freedoms".

I believe that this report is an excellent starting point and we need to

---

[95] Burris, S., et. al. "Assessing Legal Responses to COVID-19", SSRN, 2 September 2020. Short URL: https://bit.ly/2ETzgQc.

study it for the many other insights we can derive from it, but it doesn't go far enough. The very use of emergency powers in peacetime is unjustified. Only a constitutional remedy can work. I believe Australia needs to impose a constitutional restriction on peacetime emergency powers for all governments, whether state or Commonwealth.

We cannot let governments use public health as an excuse to brutalise citizens and destroy their right to occupation (shutting down shops and businesses) – effectively confiscating their property rights; as well as brutalising people by restricting their right to movement, to cross borders or even to breathe.

7.2 Expunge the precautionary principle from all legislation

There are so many problems with the precautionary principle, it is hard to know where to begin. It feeds on our fears and hysterias. That should be more than enough to reject it. But in doing so it actively asks governments to throw out their thinking brain and to do absolutely anything they wish. Anything. It is no less – and perhaps even more – dangerous than unrestrained emergency power.

This principle has not only caused devastation in environmental legislation, it is found in the Victorian *Public Health and Wellbeing Act 2008*. Section 6 of the Act states: "Precautionary principle: If a public health risk poses a serious threat, lack of full scientific certainty should not be used as a reason for postponing measures to prevent or control the public health risk".

This means the Victorian CHO did have to wait for *any* proofs to start off his mass human experiment of lockdowns in Melbourne that violates the Nuremberg Code. It doesn't matter to the precautionary principle if there is no "full scientific certainty" about lockdowns. It doesn't matter that lockdowns have been repeatedly rejected in the science. It doesn't matter if lockdowns are not in Victoria's pandemic plan. If our CHO can dream up this "remedy" one fine day, he is empowered by this principle to impose it anyway. And without *any* checks or balances on his discretionary and absolute powers. After all, he is not required to justify measures for which there is no "full scientific certainty" – these being merely a figment of his fertile imagination. And what proofs could possibly be given, anyway, for quack "remedies" like lockdowns that can only work only in someone's sick imagination? Parliamentarians can keep begging the CHO for proof but he is not obliged to even respond.

A future Royal Commission should identify whether this principle was used at any stage by the Victorian Government to abandon its well-thought out, rationally created plans.

Most scares in human history have turned out to be false. For example, in 1981 it was said that coffee causes 50 per cent of pancreatic cancers. But the scientists who made this claim retracted it in 1986. Despite that, the International Agency for Research on Cancer took till 2016 to reverse its claim that coffee is a possible cause of cancer.

It is when governments get involved in scares that things can take a sinister turn. Vast amounts of public money can be then wasted or irrational prohibitions imposed. We have seen that in loads with this Great Hysteria.

The only way to stop this madness is to use reason and a cost-benefit test. The cost-benefit test is hated by all bureaucrats and Ministers, but it is invaluable in imposing a crucial discipline on them. Else they can go haywire in no time as we have seen during this pandemic. The totally unjustified rules imposed (such as mandatory masks outdoors which have not a shred of proof) are a vivid example of such whimsy that bothers me intensely the moment I step out of my home.

The cost-benefit test is particularly well suited to dealing with scares.

Its demand for unequivocal proof of harm (or at least the best available proof of harm) and analysis of scenarios with different levels of risk can help determine a reasonable and prudent way forward. Since the overwhelming majority (maybe around 99.99%) of scares will end up being found to have been exaggerated, it is crucial to keep governments on a very tight leash.

The precautionary principle was introduced in the 1990s. Perhaps its best-known formulation – in relation to the environment – is Principle 15 of the 1992 Rio Declaration which states: "In order to protect the environment, the precautionary approach shall be widely applied by States according to their capabilities. Where there are threats of serious or irreversible damage, lack of full scientific certainty shall not be used as a reason for postponing cost-effective measures to prevent environmental degradation".

This exhorts governments (the "States") to act vigorously if they suspect something *may* go wrong. A suspicion is enough. It doesn't require governments to understand the harm thoroughly or even be sure that it will eventuate. It doesn't say that governments must undertake better quality scenario analysis and pick the option with the greatest net benefit (or, in the case of a pandemic, with the least harm) to society. Instead, it is effectively an appeal to discard reason and *carte blanche* for strong and unlimited capricious action.

The precautionary principle gives governments the freedom to only count benefits (e.g. the alleged benefits of renewable energy or the lives allegedly saved from lockdowns) and ignore costs, or to only count imagined costs (e.g. in the case of GM technology) while ignoring benefits. This principle reverses the burden of proof of harm for regulatory intervention. It undermines reason and the Enlightenment itself, taking us to the Dark Ages. It is impossible to argue with the precautionary principle because it specifically excludes the use of logic.

By exploiting our fears, the precautionary principle gives the power over our choices and decisions not only to governments that are hungry for power, but to unaccountable bureaucracies (in this case the public health bureaucracy that has smashed even the medical profession's basic training and Hippocratic Oath). Frankenstein's monster comes to mind. The precautionary principle is how we create the monster.

This principle has been a godsend for the left after the fall of communism. The beauty of the precautionary principle for the socialists is that lets them occupy the moral high ground while they demand complete control over society.

We need to not just eject the precautionary principle from Victoria but throw it out of all legislation across Australia.

7.3 Review commonwealth powers

I have an Australian passport. It doesn't say I am citizen only of Victoria. But the Commonwealth has been no friend of the people of Australia during the Great Hysteria.

The virus is a biosecurity matter, squarely within its jurisdiction. Section 51(ix) of the Australian Constitution gives this power explicitly to the Commonwealth.

Section 5 of the *Biosecurity Act 2015* prohibits any attempt to eliminate a virus. "The Appropriate Level of Protection (or ALOP) for Australia is a high level of sanitary and phytosanitary protection aimed at reducing biosecurity risks to a very low level, but not to zero".

Section 32 of the Biosecurity Act specifies that: "the manner in which the power is to be exercised is no more restrictive or intrusive than is required in the circumstances; if the power is to be exercised in relation to an individual – that the power is no more restrictive or intrusive than is required in the circumstances; if the power is to be exercised during a period – that the period is only as long as is necessary".

The same old good stuff is here as well: Don't be a maniac. Don't be intrusive. Don't be a capricious dictator.

And yet we have seen the PM, Scott Morrison, implicitly agree to Daniel Andrews's strategy (I say implicitly, since no one has done us the courtesy to tell us exactly what they are doing) and allow the harshest control measure imaginable – that violate the principles of ethics, proportionality, risk assessment, and human rights.

Apart from section 51(x) of the Constitution, Section 109 of the Australian Constitution could have been invoked to ensure that States do not take actions that are inconsistent with the laws of Australia.

The national Constitution must prohibit a peacetime state of emergency for any government (including the Commonwealth Government). But in addition, biosecurity laws need to be reviewed to ensure that no Australian is subject to public health terrorism ever again.

The Federal government must not just be able to direct State governments in such cases, the Governor General should have the power to dismiss a State Premier who disobeys. Federal armed forces must also be authorised to be used in the kind of extreme case we are seeing this time around. But all this must be thought out in advance and made first into law.

7.4 Enact a law in Victoria to criminalise public health terrorism

Victoria's public health laws need to be significantly amended.

The provisions to require information to be provided to the people need to be strengthened so we get to see the *entire* "workings", not just the final decision of the CHO – and to ensure that no CHO can disobey this mandate (as the CHO has been doing to other public health law mandates so far, and continues to do so during this Great Hysteria). The CHO must also be compelled to conduct and publish a cost-benefit analysis of options where the impact on any sector of the economy exceeds a threshold amount, say $2 million per year. The analysis doesn't have to be perfect, just a one-page table listing the pros and cons can do but must be published within two days.

We must ensure at all times that actions by the CHO are reasonable, proportionate and otherwise justified.

But much more important, it is necessary to enact a provision to criminalise the issue of any public health directive (including any Ministers who support it publicly) that ends up harming a person either directly or indirectly. And compensation provisions should be strengthened to include even mental harms, such as any depression, self-harm, domestic violence or even divorce directly precipitated by directives such as extended lockdowns.

7.5 Ethics control over government advertising

During this period, government advertising was extraordinarily one-sided – designed to ratchet up the panic to the highest level. This must not be allowed to happen again.

I dislike the idea of creating more new posts but I believe we need an Ethics Commissioner to approve all government advertising, or at least to have his views clearly and *boldly* stated in the beginning and end of an advertisement in case he dissents with it.

An Ethics Commissioner would have demanded proofs for the kind of hysteria that was being drummed up by the government. That would have reduced the madness to some extent.

7.6 Review the hiring and firing arrangements for the senior executive service

Our senior civil servants have not behaved like civil servants this time, but like Ministerial Advisers.

If I were Premier, I would expect to be advised by the civil service on all the laws and all the restrictions imposed on my powers, so as not to exceed the mandate vested in me by the people. I might want my Ministerial Advisers to tell me if my polling is good but I would want the civil service to advice purely on the basis of the laws.

Moreover, if Victoria's senior civil servants did indeed provide independent advice on the lines I have outlined in this book and that advice was rejected by the Daniel Andrews Government, then it was their moral duty, their obligation as citizens sworn to protect and advance the interests of all Victorians, to resign. None has resigned, suggesting to me that their advice has been political. They have betrayed the people of Victoria.

For more than twenty years, I have been persuaded that the New Public Management approach – in adopting which Australia led the world in the 1990s – was the better way to deliver an agile, fearless and effective bureaucracy. I have written much over the years in support of contractual arrangements for hiring and firing senior civil servants.

But during this sorry episode the senior bureaucrats forgot their role. They imagined their role is to obey the government.

A new system has to be designed. A compromise will need to be found between having a permanent senior civil service (of the sort to which

I belonged in India) and a flexible and agile system that recognises and promotes merit. The moment there is the any whiff, the slightest whiff at any stage of his or her career, that a civil servant is not providing independent, forthright professional advice, there must be immediate consequences. We must weed out subservient, spineless and self-interested bureaucrats at the earliest opportunity.

Maybe we need the Public Service Commissioner to play a direct role in monitoring the intellectual integrity of senior officials.

7.7 Let doctors decide the medicine they want to administer

The over-reach of government powers in the field of science must be reviewed, particularly when there are multiple views because different studies show different results. It is, in any case, inappropriate to mandate a single medicinal philosophy or approach.

Adam Smith and Milton Friedman wrote vigorously against government-created monopolies in the medical profession. We need to revisit these arguments and strike the right balance.

There is a strong case to be made that the governments in Australia must never interfere in the judgement of trained medical practitioners, who must have the freedom to dispense drugs they believe are suitable for their patients. Patients must consent – that should be enough. We the patients are citizens, not battery hen.

7.8 Prohibit all forms of government surveillance

This pandemic has raised another alarming issue: the "app" to allegedly track the virus but which was the most intrusive surveillance tool imaginable. Health "experts" seem to think they have unbridled power to intrude into people's lives. They do not. They must not have such powers.

7.9 Create a Black Hat Commissioner to stop public service groupthink

The armed forces are hierarchical and obedience-based. In the public service, however, everyone is paid to use their brain and to challenge anything that doesn't seem right. That is how they are supposed to provide value to the society, not by blindly obeying their Ministers or bosses.

This time, though, the public service took on the role of blind obedience. This is not the first time I have seen groupthink in the public service – it is a chronic problem in every field of public policy. Public servants often misrepresent the research. They are unable to understand complex issues correctly. They are unable to undertake basic calculations, leave alone advanced maths. They cherry-pick studies that support the preferences of their Minister. They hire consultants who will provide them with a pre-determined "finding".

To remedy this, I have long advocated (within the Treasury to my bosses) a Black Hat Commissioner. Such an official's role will be exclusively to look at the opposing arguments in any public debate, to dig into the evidence for any claims (such as, in this case, for lockdowns or masks outdoors) and to present his independent findings to the Parliament.

This will involve digging into the footnotes of government publications to determine whether a relevant study is being represented accurately. For instance, the IPCC has always provided a rather modest recommendation regarding climate change, but policy makers have used the unhinged claims of extremist and alarmist "scientists" instead of actually reading the cautions in the IPCC's own reports. Bjørn Lomborg's recent book, *False Alarm* – which I have discussed in one of my recent articles[96], shows how badly policy makers have misrepresented IPCC's findings.

---

[96] Sabhlok, Sanjeev, "Pandemic, climate change: Why is the sky always falling on our head?", *Times of India*, 6 August 2020. Short URL: https://bit.ly/3l9HL9r.

This role will require extremely high-level critical thinking skills and a wide repertoire of knowledge. It is an activist role in which the foundations of key government policies will be tested under a blowtorch.

Had such a role existed in Victoria, this mass hysteria would have been grounded within two weeks.

7.10 Clarify the nature of a public servant's voice in social media

A VPS employee is able to be a member of a political party. He or she is also able to contest State government elections without resigning the role.[97]

The main restriction on VPS employees at present is to not speak publicly (e.g. on social media) about matters on which an employee is directly advising the government. Beyond that there is a grey area (e.g. the requirement that "personal comments do not compromise their ability to perform their public sector role in an unbiased manner" – So who decides whether a VPS employee's ability is being compromised – a member of the public, the person's manager, the ruling party?).

I do not believe the law intends that a public servant cannot, in his or her private capacity, speak about matters that relate to his diverse interests as a private citizen that may lead at least to the "indirect" criticism of the government of the day.

I would like the Victorian Public Service Commissioner to call all records pertaining to my case and provide a direction to public servants in Victoria on such matters in the future, with appropriate case studies. If necessary, the Commissioner should recommend changes in the law to

---

[97] Victorian Public Service Commissioner, "Victorian Public Sector Employees Standing for Election FAQs". Short URL: https://bit.ly/2RZh9LE.

clarify matters directly in the Public Administration Act.

There is a fundamental issue at stake here: about the role of a public servant as a citizen. I believe a much more tightly and circumscribed restriction can be prescribed in the Code of Conduct to prevent the risk that someone who even indirectly criticises a government policy in an area that falls well outside his direct area of work is then directed to remove such comments.

7. 11. Large-scale working from home is unsuitable for the public service

There has been a lot of talk about WFH becoming more embedded in the workplace going forward. And it seems there are some positive benefits to be derived from it.

But there are many significant harms from WFH which may defeat the very purpose why an organisation exists, particularly a public sector organisation whose job is to provide the best – and possibly dissenting – advice to the government of the day.

Groupthink

WFH massively increases the level of groupthink in an organisation.

In the normal course of affairs, the Treasury is a fabulous place to work because of its collegiate organisational culture. There is a hierarchy that all bureaucracies have, but the edges of this hierarchy are soft.

This ensures that all views are freely exchanged. Informal conversations in the kitchen or in the lift between persons at all levels of the hierarchy are not limited to social affairs but dip into policy issues. These one-minute elevator pitches, maybe summarising a concern with the way a government is doing something, cannot be replaced by an expectation that employees will pick up the phone from home to raise a matter with a boss (who has maybe, and in writing, already rejected the concern). In the normal course, I am used to stepping over any "recalcitrant" boss to go all over the organisation to meet people who matter. The zig-zag of relationships and "politics" in a real organisation is impossible to re-create in a WFH environment. The civil service then increasingly starts behaving like an armed force.

No nanny bosses, please
From the moment WFH started there must have been a directive from senior management to focus on the mental health of the staff. At the team meetings (which increased dramatically in frequency) half the conversation was about mollycoddling the staff. Attempts to pose serious questions were skilfully steered away.

People who work in the public service are citizens in their own right. They do not go to work to be mollycoddled. They do not need a nanny. They need their organisation to do the job it is paid to do: namely, to ask the hard questions and to keep advising the Ministers about the dangers of bad policy – and to never relent on this basic duty.

Flexible work arrangements are good, but in moderation. The Treasury (and the public service more generally) must set a clear expectation that employees will work for most of their time from the workplace.

In economics we study agglomeration effects, which are similar in nature. They are undefined and fuzzy but drive many, if not most, quality improvements and innovation. A knowledge economy needs people to work in close proximity much of the time. There is a lot of body language, a lot of one-minute conversations, a lot of overhearing conversations that WFH cannot replicate.

7.12 Prohibit false and misleading data on cases and deaths

This pandemic has brought out all the bad data that could possibly be cooked up. The problems with the PCR tests (and serological tests as well) are acute but the media and the politicians put out these highly suspect data as if these were real. Likewise, the data on COVID-19 deaths can only be classified as *grossly* misleading.

Suspect data of this type must either be prohibited from being published by government bodies or they must qualify its limitations in bold each time they use it publicly, and also in every press briefing in which they cite the suspect data. There must be punishments and penalties built into the laws for those who mislead the people.

7.13. Other possible legislative measures

There will surely be many other issues requiring action that will emerge from the Great Hysteria. Some people have called for an examination of whether people should be able to initiate a recall of the government in the manner that certain states in the USA can.

I think that a recall might be impractical during a mass hysteria, particularly one like this in which the people support a misguided policy because of their fear. However, a measure like this could potentially cause a government to hesitate from imposing unnecessary restrictions.

7. 14. Reset the discipline of epidemiology

Now let me step out of the examination of the role of governments and dwell for a moment on a matter of deep concern – the nature and methods of the discipline of epidemiology.

When I started looking at epidemiological models initially in March 2020, I had assumed that this discipline was sensible enough. I then chanced upon Richard Epstein's cautionary tale. Sadly, Epstein has turned out to be right. Epidemiological modelling often has little to do with reality. Most models are nothing but "garbage in-garbage out".

The problem with models: R0
Why do models fail? The concept of R0 that is crucial to modelling is not just challenging to calculate, its early estimates are guaranteed to be misleading.

R0 is determined by the combination of transmissibility (i.e., probability of infection given contact between a susceptible and infected individual), the average rate of contact between susceptible and infected individuals, and the duration of infectiousness. Each of these determining variables are practically impossible to estimate for a small group, let alone for an entire population. We have seen earlier how difficult it is for viral loads to be sufficient. Thereafter, the level of immunity people may have to a virus varies not just by the individual but by country, by culture, by the seasons. How can all these complex matters be possibly modelled correctly?

A 2007 paper, "Theory versus Data: How to Calculate R0?" by Breban warned us that "obtaining R0 from empirical contact tracing data collected by epidemiologists and using this R0 as a threshold parameter for a population-level model could produce extremely misleading estimates". A 2011 paper entitled, "The Failure of R0" by Jing Li was equally critical: "If R0 is to be used, it must be accompanied by caveats about the method of calculation, underlying model assumptions and evidence that it is actually a threshold. Otherwise, the concept is meaningless".

Wrong on both ends of a pandemic

Epidemiology is wrong at the beginning of a pandemic because R0 can't be meaningfully used.

But the even more wicked – and to me rather unexpected – problem of epidemiology seems to be identifying a pandemic's end. During this pandemic only independent thinkers like Michael Levitt have called out the end (or the nearing of the end) at a stage when everyone else, including Anders Tegnell, was holding their breath. I wrote to Johan Giesecke months ago, asking Sweden to open up and declare the end of the pandemic. They still haven't done that.

So, we have extreme pessimism on the one end (at the beginning of a pandemic) and extreme caution at the other end. Why is this discipline not able to tell us about the mostly likely path of our pandemics?

Ethics, humility, wisdom

Many other disciplines also have this problem of tunnel vision (let me mention in passing climate science, urban planning, environment, education and health), but none has caused so much harm to mankind in 2020 as the discipline of epidemiology. It is alright to be an expert with a single-minded focus but it is not alright to forget that people are not just numbers but are fully functioning individuals with all the rights that mankind has fought hard for centuries to obtain.

There seem to be two types of epidemiologists: those with good judgement and a sense of proportion; and those without such restraint. The ones with good judgement appear to have received medical training – people like Anders Tegnell and John Ioannidis. A few other sensible ones also exist, but they seem to be so mainly due to their personal character.

But there a number of others, mostly trained in mathematical models, who are ignorant about the most basic ethical matters. I repeatedly provided feedback to one such scientist against mass testing, not just from the economic but from the ethical and privacy angle. He brushed me aside. Many such single-minded epidemiologists have been obsessed with the curves, the spread of the disease and estimating this or that, while recommending the most draconian measures possible that are marked by their refusal to consider the ethics, the impact or the proportionality of these measures.

I invite epidemiologists to study F.A. Hayek's Nobel lecture[98] and his book, *The Fatal Conceit*. Economics, as a branch of moral philosophy, has struggled with the infinitely complex problems which epidemiology must now begin to explore. There is a lot that invisible to most of us, that we need to be able to see.

That is why I call my book on economics for children (might I add that it has been praised by the economics Nobel laureate Vernon Smith and is also freely available for download[99]), *Seeing the Invisible*. The world is complex. We need to look behind the obvious. And economics teaches humility. We may not like what others do but they have the God given right to do what they please as long as they don't physically harm others.

Plato and Aristotle wrote about *phronesis*, the wisdom, judgement and ethics that leads to the common good. Such wisdom has been reflected almost ethereally in Anders Tegnell's actions and speech. At a minimum, epidemiologists need to learn moral philosophy and economics. A few months ago, I outlined a course content for a new epidemiology. I am happy to work with epidemiology departments to share these suggestions and show them how they can try to regain my respect.

---

[98] Nobel Prize. Friedrich von Hayek Prize Lecture. 11 December 1974. Short URL: https://bit.ly/3I59LuP.

[99] Sabhlok, Sanjeev, *Seeing the Invisible* (2018). Short URL: https://bit.ly/2EVpGwn.

8
Conclusion

- After a full year of this pandemic, we have had *less than a week* of additional deaths from COVID-19 that are over and above the 60 million that occur ordinarily from all other causes, each year.
- The novel coronavirus pandemic is not a 1 in 100-year event but is closer to a 1 in 30-year event. My ballpark estimate is that this pandemic is at least 50 times less lethal than the Spanish flu and is likely to end up around 100 times less lethal. Further, by protecting the elderly, most COVID-19 deaths can be averted.
- The scientific literature on pandemics has considered public health measures for pandemics for decades. Science has repeatedly and outright rejected the concept of lockdowns which are considered to be a menace. The WHO's 2019 guidelines on managing pandemics do not recommend lockdowns "in any circumstances".
- All Australian governments had pandemic plans. These were focused on risk and proportionality. No plan included heavy-handed measures like 5-kilometre prisons, 23-hour curfews, prohibition on ordinary social interactions (equivalent to solitary confinement for some), masks outdoors or shutting down Melbourne to wait forever for a vaccine.

- We need a Royal Commission to find out why these approved plans, prepared at great taxpayer cost, were abandoned within days of the onset of the pandemic.

- Instead, repressive *experimental* measures previously rejected, such as lockdowns and mandatory masks outdoors – with these new experimental measures never approved by any ethics committee or justified to the people – were introduced. The over-zealous police force with its newly founded powers and meted out brutal punishment to innumerable ordinarily law-abiding citizens, creating a full-blown Police State.

- In doing so, a wide range of State, Commonwealth and international laws were ignored including the specific prohibition found in the Victorian *Public Health and Wellbeing Act 2008* on the exercise of arbitrary power by a Chief Health Officer.

- Overzealous suppression of the virus (perhaps even elimination – a comprehensive and prosecutable breach of biosecurity law) was attempted without disclosing the objective. ICUs across Australia remained largely empty.

- The elderly were ignored, not protected fiercely, leading to hundreds of avoidable deaths.

- These heavy-handed measures that attack civil liberties and human rights and violate the Nuremberg Code, are imposing catastrophic direct and indirect costs on society that have not been publicly identified and published by governments, let alone considered as part of any consultative decision-making process.

- There is a very significant and fundamental difference between loss of life arising from an Act of Nature (e.g. virus) and from an Act of Man (e.g. lockdowns). Governments are not authorised – by analogy – to burn down additional homes and kill unaffected people in order to save those who might be at risk of being engulfed in a bushfire.

- Evidence of the catastrophic collateral damage of lockdowns is pouring in every day. Among others: suicides, deaths from not seeking urgently needed medical attention (leading to additional cancer and heart disease), increased stillbirths, children harming themselves, domestic abuse murders, a rise in homelessness, and increased alcohol and drug abuse. The longer the lockdowns go on the worse this damage will get.

We need to:

- **Immediately** revert to Victoria's original risk-and proportionality-based pandemic plan and strictly follow the laws. All lockdowns and unnecessary restrictions must be immediately lifted, including the opening up of *all* borders. Note that this is not a plea to "let it rip". Instead, public health guidance and recommendations should be issued for voluntary compliance. The government should put 80% of its pandemic resources on protecting the elderly. Private industry should be guided to adopt a risk-based approach. Highly targeted quarantines of a short, medically approved duration should be used to keep hospitalisations within ICU capacity.

- **In the medium and longer term**, implement constitutional and legal reforms to ensure that the widescale public health terrorism witnessed in 2020 across all parts of Australia doesn't occur again; criminalise the acts of Ministers or their authorised representatives who cause, through public health measures that they impose, *even a single additional death*; and expunge the precautionary principle from all legislation.